Twentieth-Century Painting

Compass History of Art

Edited by André Held and D. W. Bloemena

The complete series includes:

Twentieth-Century Painting

Dr. H. L. C. Jaffé

University lecturer in Modern Art at Amsterdam University

THE VIKING PRESS
New York

A COMPASS BOOKS original edition

Published in 1963 by The Viking Press, Inc.

625 Madison Avenue, New York 22, N.Y.

Library of Congress catalog card number: 63–12645

Printed in Holland.

Contents

Author's Note

The concept of reality, as it is used in this book, should be interpreted in the widest sense of the word in the way that Vincent van Gogh described it in a letter to his brother Theo (from Arles, dated 3 September 1888): 'I always hope to make a discovery there [in painting], to express the love of two lovers by a wedding of two complementary colours, by their mingling and their opposition, and the mysterious vibrations of kindred tones … to express hope by a star, eagerness of soul by a sunset radiance. Certainly there is no deceptive realism in that, but isn't it something that actually exists?'

Twentieth-Century Painting

Introduction

It seems an impossible task to consider the art of the twentieth century – the century we live in, whose second third is still not over – from a single, unified standpoint. A common denominator could be found for the European art (particularly the painting) of earlier centuries. Different stylistic concepts have been deduced from the different ages, usually equated with centuries, and the changes in them have been traced in connexion with changes in human culture; rhythms and breaks in the historical development of visual art have been discerned. But, when it comes to describing, interpreting and weighing our own age, the whole arsenal of critical and historical ideas seems to be inadequate. Not only do we lack the distance in time without which a wider survey is impossible, but the multiplicity and variety of the phenomena which are crowded into the short historical space of the last seventy-five years seem to condemn to failure any unified approach to this period.

Nevertheless, in this book I will attempt to view the development of visual art, and above all painting, from a single standpoint, and from one which by no means starts out from the often contradictory formal characteristics of contemporary art, but tries to demonstrate the common intellectual content in this very variety of formal characteristics. The question that must be asked at the beginning of any attempt to view twentieth-century painting as a whole concerns the 'laws it follows' – in other words, the principles that determine its form and essence and govern its development at every stage. The studies of the last hundred years have shown that these are not scientific laws prescribing the germination, maturity and decline of each artistic trend, but rather a reflection of man's outlook on life at the time – which is why for some seventy years they have been thought of as a 'will to form'.

What, then, is this law, this 'will to form' which is equally valid for every trend of the art of this century, and which is closely, essentially bound up with the outlook of our age? Perhaps it can best be put into words as the question of the essence of reality. No other period of European painting has asked this question so clearly and decisively; no other period has, in the same way, made it the most important concern of its artistic thought and aims.

Admittedly the Netherlandish painters of the fifteenth century and the Spanish and Dutch schools of the baroque age investigated reality to an extent never imagined before, and their voyages of discovery into unknown regions influenced painting for many generations – but the discovery of reality was not the only law behind their painting; above all, reality had not yet become a problem for these painters. It was in fact the nineteenth century which took the decisive steps towards sub-jugating painting to this law, this criterion – but it was not until the end of that century that this development was first fully revealed.

Truth and Reality

Despite its introduction in the nineteenth century it was not until this century that the problem of reality became central for visual art. Not until this period of history, after painting had slowly freed itself from all its ties with religion, history, scholarship and technical curiosity, could the question become decisive. For the first time, now that man had lost the security of religion, myths and the hierarchic order, he was confronted by reality: it became a problem, a challenge, and consequently the preoccupation of man's thought and feeling. At the end of the nine-teenth century painting became in fact, and explicitly, a view of life, a *Weltanschauung*, in the most literal sense: the artist viewed the world in order to give an account of its reality content, its truth.

The new attitude of painting could be recognized in a number of symp-toms. One of the most striking was the change in the stock of themes after the middle of the nineteenth century: subjects such as the altarpiece, the historical painting, mythological and Biblical figure compositions, disappeared over the years, to be replaced first by landscape (as the great confrontation of nature) and then by scenes from daily life, now completely free from the narrative emphasis of earlier works. Finally the centre of the stage was taken by still life in which, at the end of the nineteenth century, the whole problem of the essence of reality was concentrated. And now it became plain that the artist was not satisfied with mere appearance; he was looking beyond visual perception and trying to find the essence and meaning of reality.

The distinction between perception and reality constitutes the problem of the painting of this period, and the causes of this schism were numerous and of very different kinds. The general movement away from the positivist view of reality was undoubtedly a basic factor – particularly if we are thinking of an anonymous 'will to form' linked to the period. This trend is embodied most clearly in Gustave Courbet's painting and is best described in his own words: 'La peinture est un art essentiellement concret et ne peut consister que dans la représentation des choses réelles et existantes. Un objet abstrait, non visible, non existant, n'est pas du domaine de la peinture'. Here the perception of the senses is relied on exclusively to give a consciousness of reality, so that reality and perception are equated with each other.

But it was not long before the progress of science, which positivism cherished as an ideal, had cast doubt on this equation and destroyed the indestructible belief in the reality of visual perception. The very fact that science could reveal a reality which the eyes were only slowly beginning to penetrate but which the mind can deduce, to a large extent, by means of inferences and conjectures – this very fact was bound to undermine the apparent certainty of the positivist view of reality. In addition there was the rebellious feeling of a new generation of artists who refused to register, passively, what they saw and on the contrary thought it the artist's task to give shape to an idea of reality, in a positive act of creation.

At the historical moment when Courbet was painting his most nearly perfect pictures and so giving the positivist outlook its most convincing embodiment, another quite opposite conception of reality began to occupy and disturb the minds of contemporary artists and thinkers. In the art criticism and essays on the art of his time published by the great poet and critic Charles Baudelaire in the middle of the century, there emerged for the first time a clear intimation that along with (or indeed underneath) the positive, tangible reality there might be another, essential reality: the reality which is not bound up with the material, the painting, and so is accessible to neither the eye nor the hand, but only to the imagination, the lively mind of man. In his aesthetics of the non-natural, the artificially created, Baudelaire laid the foundations of a conception of the world and of man's part in it whose significance was not to be fully revealed until the twentieth century.

It was Baudelaire too who for the first time drew attention, with great clarity, to a phenomenon which was of decisive importance for visual art towards the end of the nineteenth century and the beginning of the twentieth: the invention and development of photography. This historic event, which Baudelaire was the first to connect with the history of art, was to have the effect of an Industrial Revolution on the art of the following years, a revolution which undoubtedly had no less an influence on painting than the invention of printing just four centuries earlier.

For what in fact had happened? Previously, in the period before this invention, anyone who wished to preserve something for posterity, to record its features and unique quality, could only go to the artist to fulfil this wish. From the time that the 'portrait' was invented it had remained the concern, the task of the artist – either the painter or the sculptor. I use the word 'portrait' to include the capturing of the individual features of any object – a person, a house, an animal, a ship, a landscape, or indeed still life laid out on a table.

But, with the arrival of photography, anybody who wanted to preserve a likeness in this way could also call on the photographer's services, or even photograph the object with his own camera. So man's scientific progress had made a decisive difference to the frontiers of the artist's domain: the whole territory of the portrait, which had previously been part of the uncontested empire of the creative artist, was now banished to the realm of mere reportage. Many artists, in particular many painters of the young generation just before and around the turn of the century, felt this curtailment of their empire as a challenge: reality, the essential truth of nature and man's environment, was just what the camera was not in a position to capture. Reality and what the eye sees are not identical: the eye (or its mechanical substitute, the camera) is not adequate by itself to capture reality pictorially. An act of the mind is necessary too. It is in the light of these facts that we should understand the following pronouncement by Paul Klee; it may be taken as symptomatic of the painting of the twentieth century and its idea of reality: 'Art does not reproduce what can be seen: it makes things visible.'

If we accept these words as characteristic of the painting of the twentieth century, then the idea undoubtedly began before the turn of the century. The dialectical development which began with the use of photography and the overestimation of the perceived image stemmed from an idea of reality such as is embodied in Courbet's pictures and his conception of painting – the idea that reality and what the eyes see are identical. But painting soon moved away from this vision of reality: Manet subordinated reality to the act of perceiving it and made his eye the sole judge of it.

The Impressionists

In the very next generation – the Impressionists – the line of development begins to bend. Admittedly, the Impressionists are always presented as the exponents of an optimistic *joie de vivre*, as painters who, in bright, glowing colours, sing exaltingly of a life of delight. And this idea is undoubtedly correct. But the art of the Impressionists (of Monet, say, or Pissarro, Renoir or Sisley) had another side too: in them the depreciation of material things is conspicuous. This emerges most clearly in Claude Monet's late works which were painted in series – *St Lazare, The Façade of Rouen Cathedral, The Poplars*, the *Haystacks*, the views of Venice and London, and finally *The Water Lilies*. In these works Monet painted a number of pictures of the same subject, but with different light in each case. And this approach to painting in itself shows that the object painted, the actual subject of the painting, had lost its value and become only a pretext for depicting the light. The light – the most intangible, immaterial phenomenon in all nature – is the real subject of these pictures; their apparent subject gives them only a name. The things which appear in these pictures are dissolved by the light; they have become coloured shadows which are only called into constantly changing life by the ever-changing light. In this art little is left of the concrete substance of objects, of their own, autonomous existence, as Courbet understood it. As had happened once before, at the end of the period of classical antiquity, Impressionism, by depreciating the world of material things, caused the old vision of the world to be extensively destroyed; it also hastened the emergence of new forms in a decisive way. For man's increasing self-awareness was revealed in the way the Impressionist painters translated a subjective vision into an immaterial, barely tangible impression and captured this on canvas.

But hardly had Impressionism aroused a reponse in wider circles than criticism of its principles was voiced, coming mainly from the ranks of the painters themselves. The description of Claude Monet, a mixture of admiration and criticism, which has been attributed to Paul Cézanne – 'Monet, ce n'est qu'un oeil, mais quel oeil!' – is typical of this reaction. This concise summing-up shows clearly that the criticism of contemporaries – at least, the progressive elements among them – was directed chiefly against the all-dominant sensuality of this art, against the lack of any intellectual act. What the younger painters found fault with in the painting of the Impressionist masters was, indeed, the fact that their painting, which registered every nuance of the transitory moment with senses sharpened to the utmost was unable to offer a true picture of a more permanent and meaningful reality. And the painters who risked trying to capture a new and different reality towards the end of the nineteenth century all came from the Impressionist circle. They were seeking a more comprehensive, stable and deeply rooted reality than the product of mere visual perception, than all the sensual and visual observations the eye could apprehend in a fleeting moment.

Forerunners of the Twentieth Century

Between 1880 and 1890 a few painters who offered an alternative vision to that of the Impressionists – Cézanne, van Gogh, Gauguin, Rousseau, Redon, Seurat – broke away from the Impressionist school. Each of these six great painters, of course, viewed the world in a different way, but they had one characteristic in common: in their conception of reality none of them allowed themselves to rely merely on the passive record of the senses. All of them viewed the creation of a personal vision of the world as an intellectual act, an achievement of the human will and its power of creativity. These six painters, then, became the ancestors of twentieth-century painting. The painting of this century owes a particularly large debt to Cézanne and van Gogh – two great artists. In the complete contrast between the characteristics and artistic aims of the two men we see again a polarity which has ruled the destiny of painting in so many art-periods, most recently before them in the antithesis between Ingres and Delacroix.

Both Cézanne and van Gogh were looking for a reality which would extend beyond the transitory appearance of the moment: Cézanne thought to find it by mental discipline, van Gogh by the inspiration of emotion. And in this choice, suited to the character and mental outlook of each of them, the two great masters of the dying century pointed the way which the painting of the twentieth century was to follow and along which it would find new regions still closed to the nineteenth century's conception of reality.

Cézanne [1, 2]

Cézanne overcame the fortuitousness of the Impressionist outlook, the arbitrariness of a conception based purely on what the eye sees, by means of his strict, clear, and simple theory of method. He was a man of Latin stamp, who wanted to establish the structure and regularity of reality. He was concerned to 'give reality the permanence of the eternal' – and so was not satisfied with the chance moment. And the means he used towards this end was the discipline of the human mind. This is why he started from the laws of geometry (intellectual and therefore abstract) and strove to reduce the whole of nature's cornucopia of forms to the simplest stereometric bodies – the sphere, the cone, the prism. In this way he wrote the grammar of the language of the new painting, built up a kind of architecture of the picture which enabled the painting of the next generation to claim the right to an autonomous existence of its own. To use his own words, his art is 'a harmony parallel with nature'; for the creations of the human mind stand side by side with the works of nature, of equal rank and value. Cézanne's art is a first triumph of the human mind over the variety and arbitrariness of nature which, as a creator of his own universe, he organizes, thus making it accessible to the human mind as meaningful reality. Order and regularity – these are the two principles which inhabit Cézanne's Latin painting and which he was able to deepen so that they became a meaningful interpretation of life.

Vincent van Gogh [5, 6, 7]

Vincent van Gogh, a Dutchman, pursued a completely different course: for him true reality was revealed through the glow of warm human sympathy. The following words, from a letter to his brother, are characteristic of his attitude to reality: 'Isn't it possible that one sees a thing better and more correctly if one loves it than if one doesn't?'

This bond of love linking him to his subjects – a real *unio mystica* – determined his forms and colours; he was interested not in the external likeness but in the interior, invisible truth. He wanted to learn to 'make such inaccuracies, yes, variations, transformations and alterations to the truth that they may become – yes lies, if you like, but truer than the literal truth': van Gogh wanted to paint emotion, excitement, affection – and he wanted to make these things (which did not belong to the sphere of painting in the sense of Courbet's strict demands) visible in his pictures, for they too were reality, and indeed, to this passionate painter, the decisive reality. The rhythm of his brushwork became the expression of an inner movement; in the ardour of his passion the forms of nature too took on movement – cypress trees flared up to the sky like black flames, the sun and the stars revolved with restless intensity, his whole world became the expression of a dynamic view of life inspired by passionate feeling. It is the man, the artist, who inspires the world by means of his sensibility and this gives reality meaning and significance; Vincent van Gogh created this new, meaningful and inspired reality – modelled on the experience of his own life and work.

The life and work of these two great artists, Cézanne and van Gogh, each determining a trend, represent the two poles between which the painting of the twentieth century was to develop: reality governed by reason, and reality inspired by emotion. Between them lies the whole broad territory of painting and *Weltanschauung* towards which many painters of the same generation contributed their share to the consolidation of a view of life, thus laying the foundation for the painting of the twentieth century.

Gauguin [3, 4]

In his flight from European civilization to the South Sea Isles Gauguin found a mythical reality which was his contribution to painting. The magic rites of the natives, which we in our European arrogance call 'primitive', the directness of their relationship with men and the world about them, aroused in Gauguin a feeling for a reality such as Europe had long ceased to understand: myth, as heightened reality, can in fact be truer than literal truth. Gauguin captured the directness of this experience of a reality within one's reach and yet handed down from the remoteness of prehistory with the aid of brilliantly juxtaposed colours applied in flat and often unbroken areas. His pictures are impregnated with this magical view of reality.

Le Douanier Rousseau [20]

This apparently unique primitiveness, the directness of this relationship with reality, was not only to be achieved by going to the South Sea Isles. Another artist of the same generation – Rousseau, a customs officer – was able to discover the paradise-like purity of an innocent reality in the heart of Paris and its suburbs. For him nature, man's environment, was still a miracle, revealed anew each time to his astonished eyes. Moreover his presentation of reality was completely uninfluenced by any artistic theories: he was self-taught and proud to call himself a pupil of nature. With simplicity and wonder he spelled out the things he saw around him and put them together to make words, sentences, a convincing presentation of reality. His pictures embrace a whole world, a world of familiar or fairy-tale objects which nevertheless always become miraculous in the poet's vision and, because of this characteristic, the directness of the experience, grip and thrill. For it is not everyone, nowadays, whose eyes can see reality as an intact, undisturbed whole, a cosmos: this demands that the gaze should be innocent and the surface of the soul unruffled, which is exceptional today. This view of reality can be found only in painters whose hearts are simple, artists for whom (perhaps because of their social position) reality has never become a problem.

Redon [16]

The same generation, though a completely different background, produced a painter who considerably enlarged the territory of reality. This was Odilon Redon. He was a contemporary of Monet, but his vision has little to do with the way Monet saw the world. This is evident only perhaps in the way in which Redon handles colours, giving his pictures the magic of opalescence – this is the teaching of the Impressionist school. But with these means he was trying to reach a quite different goal: he was the man who discovered the halfway country between dreams and what one sees with one's eyes. He painted figures and landscapes, and incidents, such as no man has seen when awake: his world is the reality that emerges beneath our closed eyelids, the land of visions, of dreams, of fairy-tales and fables. After an interval of many centuries, painting was once again enriched from the region that stretches out beyond what can be seen with the eye – by pictures from childhood memory, the forms and colours of the inner imagination, appearing from unknown regions of human experience. The discovery of dream-visions considerably widened the horizons of reality – for these forms and colours, which of course have no place in Courbet's formula, nevertheless do belong to our own experience as human beings. With the sensitive eye of an Impressionist painter Redon captured these dream-visions, with all their chromatic splendour and their exciting wealth of forms, in his pastels and paintings: he used the language of his generation to fashion new truths.

Seurat [8]

In the same way, Seurat began by employing the Impressionist doctrines, and using these means to pursue a different goal. The reality which he discovered and by means of which he overcame the accepted standards of the Impressionist view of the world was the actual reality of the work of art. His determined work in the studio, principally on the systemization of pictorial means, told him that a painting, a work of art, not only depicted nature but also added a certain amount of reality to nature: the composition of rising and falling lines, the harmony of contrasting and related colours, formed a new reality independent of nature. He realized that forms and colours obeyed rules similar to those of music, counterpoint and thoroughbass. Thus the artist was able to create a new, meaningful reality which – freed from all accident and arbitrariness – confronts us, permanent and purified. Seurat's intellectual achievement was to see the work of art as a compositional solution and also as an enrichment and rationalization of reality: this was the step which he took, consciously and on the basis of a new art-outlook, when he progressed from Impressionism to Neo-Impressionism. The few, but masterly, pictures which he created in his short life bear eloquent witness to this. Seurat is undoubtedly one of the 'fathers of modern art'.

The New Art of the Twentieth Century

Crisis in Standards and Values in 1900

At the turn of the century the idea of reality altered considerably. From being a positive recognition of perception and its results, it had changed (after passing through the purely sensual attitude of the Impressionists) into a problem: from the question of the nature of reality had developed the problem of whether there was a reality at all that could be grasped and how it could be grasped. The new generation was no longer satisfied with mere recognition of the facts and purely sensual perception of objects: at the beginning of the new century people began to wrestle with the *problem* of reality. By then a new generation of artists was making its voice heard and they viewed the traditional standards of the nineteenth century with mistrust. Scientific and technical discoveries, and the conclusions which the human mind had drawn from them, had greatly widened the scope of reality, but at the same time had shattered people's belief in the positive truth contained in sensual perception. So in the period round about 1900 (a period which in another respect too was characterized by a crisis of standards and values) there occurred a change which had a decisive effect on the art of our age: painting broke with the sensual perception of reality because in this perception it no longer found the truth-content on which an art could be built – an art, that is, which aimed to say something valid and undisputed about reality.

The decisive step from the revolutionary innovations of the 'fathers of modern art' (who, like Moses, saw the promised land before them but could not enter it) to the new art of the twentieth century was approached by a series of artists who were all born in the 1850s or shortly afterwards, and so were almost exact contemporaries of Vincent van Gogh: Bonnard and Vuillard in France, Ensor in Belgium, Hodler in Switzerland and Munch in Norway. The characteristic feature which all these painters share is that they give prominence to the expression of the work and use the subject, the objective fact, only as a pretext.

Bonnard [11, 12, 29], Vuillard [13, 14] and the 'Nabis'

To Bonnard and Vuillard (and indeed to the whole 'Nabi' group: these two painters were its most powerful and convincing representatives) the expression of the picture was above all the independent organization and harmony of the pictorial whole – the new reality the artist had created on his canvas. Maurice Denis, the theorist of the period, expressed the principle of this generation as follows: 'Remember that before being a horse, a nude woman, or an anecdote, a picture is essentially a flat surface covered with colours assembled in a certain order'. These words might well contain the basis for an abstract art – but such possibilities were of little importance to the Nabis: their concern was to show in their pictures that a harmony, a tightly knit pictorial reality could be attained through the painter's lyric sensitivity, the art ‚with which he interwove colours and forms on the surface, and not through the meaning of the actual subject.

It is typical of these painters that the subjects of their pictures are insignificant, of a commonplace and by no means exciting simplicity and intimacy. It is the interweaving of the colours, the harmony of form and colour, which makes their pictures works of art, and not the actual content. This lyric art, which today seems classical in its perfection, made a significant contribution towards renewing art and the feeling for reality: it re-emphasized the artist's intellectual act, his active role in the face of reality.

Ensor [17], Hodler [30] and Munch [28]

The three other great artists of this generation, Ensor, Hodler and Munch, came from the north of Europe and started from a completely different position – from the feeling of dizziness which confronting reality gave them. With Ensor this *Weltangst* took on above all the character of an obsession: space, people and things in his everyday surroundings became lurking, oppressive dangers to him, reality was a threat. Towards this reality he had 'second sight'; he saw through the enigmatic quality of objects and behind their forms discovered another, ghostly, reality which he stripped bare.

Hodler's artistic destiny confronted him with a natural scene which was grandiose, superhuman, and with a race of men which both in the past and in the present had shown the same overwhelming character. In his painting, particularly the magnificent landscapes of Lake Geneva painted in his last years, he often succeeds in banishing the last scrap of this overwhelming force from them and transposing them into human values; his artistic means are a splendid simplification of colour and form and a strict rhythm which, in his murals, both governs the human bodies and yet subordinates itself to them. His 'parallelism', the pictorial theory of parallels strengthening each other, is an intellectual feat which helps to control reality.

To Edvard Munch, the third great master of the generation, nature and man were both the source and the mirror of his *Weltangst* – a similar anguish to that expressed in Strindberg's writings. For him the whole of reality, as in van Gogh's works, is permeated by secret, invisible forces – only it is not inspired but possessed – and trying to make these forces visible is not only an artistic task but a heroic enterprise, an attempt to offer resistance to this reality, to exorcize it by looking at it and through it. His art is an effort to cure this by means of the mind. This is why his painting, unlike that of his French contemporaries, is also completely anti-classical: the dramatic, gloomy tension of his landscapes and figure-studies, often comparable with Shakespeare's plays, tries to conjure up an explanation and a solution for a cultural crisis.

In Munch's pictures reality is a conquered enemy, and it was this situation – Jacob wrestling with the angel – which became the problem of the next generation.

Revolution in Painting

By the first decade of the new century painting all over Europe was in the grip of a new trend. Consciously and resolutely, it had set itself the task of mastering reality afresh. To the artists of the new generation (most were born in about 1880) van Gogh's work was a shining example to follow, and Munch had led the way further with his struggles with reality.

They resisted the idea that an artist should follow nature and, inspired by a new and active feeling for life, aimed to wrestle with reality until it yielded its secrets and gave them its blessing. They fought to subordinate the whole of man's environment to this dynamic, enthusiastic feeling for life, and so to create a living, intellectual reality.

France: the Fauves

A group of French painters gave the first impetus to this revolution in painting – and at the same time in outlook. The leading figure in this group was Henri Matisse [32, 33, 165], although it also included Derain [35], Marquet [31], Rouault [43], Vlaminck [34] and others. They were given the name of the Fauves (the wild animals) – at first intended as an insult – shortly after their first exhibition. They tried to breathe new life and spirit into nature chiefly by using together colours that were glaring, often shriekingly discordant, with brutal contrasts ('like dynamite-charges'). With the violence of these collisions the painters attained a new liveliness, a turbulent dynamism in reality which was in striking contrast to the peaceable inoffensiveness of the landscape-art generally produced by the followers of the Impressionists. By means of colour, reality became drama, action, and intellectual statement and no longer merely a fact recorded by the artist.

German Expressionism

The fact that German Expressionism emerged at the same time shows that this current was the embodiment of an intellectual feeling which was dominating other parts of Europe as well at this period: in 1905 a number of German artists, who also belonged to the generation of 1880, formed themselves into a group called *Die Brücke* in Dresden. The enthusiasm for nature of Germany's *Sturm und Drang* period awoke to new life in the work of these young and revolutionary painters – Kirchner [39], Heckel [36], Schmidt-Rottluff [37] – and the ecstasy of life was to be reflected in their mastery over reality. As its name suggests, German Expressionism is chiefly an art of expression: it seeks to confront the impression (which the Impressionists had registered passively) with the active force of the expression of human feelings and so 'spiritualize' the world. Through the violence of the colour and the brutal distortion of forms all reality becomes a dramatic event, laden with explosive expression: trees and people writhe in paralysing anguish or stretch up ecstatically towards the skies; the very space in which this drama takes place is sometimes suffocatingly cramped, as though it has shrunk together with fear, and at other times so expansive that the edges of the picture can hardly contain it. Every form and every colour is filled with a magical inner life that dominates and distorts objects, and this life is the real content of these pictures, the apparent subject being again only a pretext. For the Brücke painters, and also for a few German Expressionists who followed individual paths, such as Emil Nolde [38] and Paula Modersohn [26], this is the basis for a new, inspired kind of painting.

The 'Blaue Reiter'

A few years later in Munich the last group of Expressionist painters emerged – the *Blaue Reiter*. In the way they experienced nature and 'intellectualized' their view of life the painters of this group – Jawlensky, [41], Kandinsky [67, 68, 126], Klee [65, 66, 144], Macke [60] and Marc [62] – went as far as the borders of abstract painting: their aim was to fuse with the laws of the universe in a mystic union. They attuned man's feeling for life to the laws of nature. This is how Franz Marc's animal pictures are to be understood; the same applies to the attempt of these painters to give expression to the harmonies of the universal soul in their pictures. It is no accident that the first abstract painting came from one of these painters: in 1910 Kandinsky dared to take this decisive step, moved by the same feelings that made Marc write 'Matter is something which the human mind suffers, at best, but does not recognize'.

Throughout Europe the Expressionists gave reality a new form and spirit. It was they too who brought us to the point where we could see distortions of form and exaggerations of colour as truth, 'truer than literal truth'.

Cubism

Braque [47, 49, 128] and Picasso [21, 46, 48, 104–105, 169]
In the dialectical development of modern painting (which had already begun at the end of the nineteenth century with the reaction against Impressionism) a new stream of painting emerged, offering an astringent and systematic order in place of more subjective, expressionist tendencies. This was Cubism, which was born in the first decade of the new century. It leant upon Cézanne's work and discoveries, but did not keep his link

with nature. Objects do, in fact, appear in Cubist paintings, a glass, a carafe, keys, jugs, a small table – figures – but they are there only to demonstrate the strict system, the grammar of the pictorial language. Braque, who with Picasso was one of the founders of Cubism, expressed the Cubist attitude towards reality with great pungency: 'The senses distort; only the mind gives form'. As befits their Latin origin, the Cubists aim at a clear picture of reality which is accessible to the reason; their vision of the world is founded not on sensual experience but on the methodical, almost mathematical understanding of the mind. And this understanding is more important than subjective experience; it can take into account the arbitrariness of any appearance and should aim at objective validity. So Cubism completely rejects a single viewpoint from which to regard an object and makes knowledge of this object completely independent of the artist's chance view of it. In Cubist pictures a given object is viewed from all round, from above and below, from the side, from in front and behind, so that the subject of the picture is not its appearance but its essence.

It is noteworthy and to the point that the Cubists, who took Cézanne's work as a model, at the beginning of their researches (1907–11) used a method similar to that which Seurat and the Neo-Impressionists had devised and used for colour – systematic analysis and splitting up. Just as the Neo-Impressionists broke down colour-effects into tiny particles of pure colour, so the Cubists dared to break down form and reduce it to tiny units of pure geometrical form. As a matter of fact, this similarity of method does not seem to be accidental: it was founded on the same scientific attitude towards reality, the urge to rely no longer merely on the chances of perception and impression but to find more assured standards based on intellectual knowledge of reality.

So the pictures from this first period of Cubism have the character, sharpness and clarity of a scientific analysis of reality. With almost anatomical precision they investigate form, its structure and laws, and quite deliberately relegate the other factor in a painter's vision – colour – to a humbler, secondary role.

These pictures are almost monochrome; there are only a few shades of grey, ochre, and green to help make form emerge in clear, spatial relief on the surface. The emphasis is on the structure and syntactical composition of forms: the facets into which each form is broken up join together, like words, to make sentences – and according to a very strict method of sentence-construction. All the forms and parts of forms are grouped round focal points so that an oval, elliptical composition emerges; it seems to huddle together, leaving the corners of the picture almost unpainted and empty. This analytical phase of Cubism produced a series of masterpieces, and indeed the new, methodical view of the world soon showed by its choice of themes that it was able to cover the whole of reality: Cubism did not confine itself to still life, the formal structure of simple objects, but also ventured on figure-compositions, portraits and landscapes. Above all it introduced into the sphere of painting invisible things, things of the mind – such as music and memory – which did not permit any other kind of treatment.

After a few years of intensive research and experiment the Cubist masters became aware that although this method of visual analysis could indeed cover the whole of reality – like a clear, defined scientific language – nevertheless, because of its formalized character, contact with living reality was in danger of being lost. The Cubist artists themselves recognized that Cubism might become a mere theory, an arid method, and so were able to avert the danger by turning back to the simplest reality and including this, directly and without alteration, in their pictures. The decisive part in this process was played by the collages which Picasso and Braque created in 1912; first typographical forms and then material actually taken from reality – paper, straw, cards, etc – were introduced into the composition. And these bits of paper stuck on to the surface play a very direct role in the pictures: because their actual substance is different from that of the painting they bring the picture out of the sphere of purely intellectual speculation back into the world of everyday reality.

Juan Gris [51]

Thus synthetic Cubism emerged. Its greatest exponent was Juan Gris, who deliberately chose the opposite path to that of the analytical method of the early years – not distilling a geometrical formula out of objects but making geometrical formulae change into objects. This is not the process of scientific investigation – this is the method of the creator, the artist, coming into its own.

De la Fresnaye [50], Léger [58, 79, 164] and Delaunay [59]

Along with these two phases, which followed each other chronologically, Cubism developed in another direction – in the realm of architecture, that is, where painting is concerned, in the realm of the mural. In this way Roger de la Fresnaye linked large surfaces to form a composition with the feeling of architecture.

And Fernand Léger's splendid compositions, whose figurative portions approach modern machines in their structure and the clarity of their forms, are filled with the same architectonic aspiration. But it was really Robert Delaunay who took the decisive step in this direction when, in his pictures shortly before the First World War, he created a colour- and light-architecture out of prismatic refractions. His method too started out from analysis, the breaking up of light, but soon arrived at a synthesis which also included the movement of light – a dynamic factor, that is – in the composition and the vision of reality.

The Italian Futurists

This tendency to dynamism, in contrast to the static, concentric principle of early Cubism, was seen elsewhere – apart from Delaunay's work and partly under its influence – in the pictures and sculptures of the Italian Futurists. Starting out from Cubism, this group of artists (Ballà [55], Boccioni [53], Carrà [54] and Severini) who came together in 1910 took the depiction of movement as their aim. For to them movement, the dynamism of modern life, was the essential reality of our age. Their construction, too, derived from splitting up, from decomposition: just as the Cubists broke up form into its parts, its facets, so the Futurists attempted to break up movement and capture its various phases together on the canvas, rather like printing the various shots in a film on top of each other. This produced a powerful suggestion of movement, which the painters of the group used chiefly to depict vehement, violent motion: racing cars, processions, the tumult of the streets – these were their favourite themes. Moreover they exploited the possibilities of showing simultaneous actions side by side, depicting the event itself and the reaction of the subject experiencing that event at the same time.

The Emergence of a New Outlook

So the investigation of reality, which had begun at the start of the century with the subjective conquests and distortions of the Expressionists, was transformed shortly after the First World War into the creation of a reality inaccessible to perception and the traditional pictorial means. Hand in hand with the emergence of a new outlook went the creation of a new pictorial language which was able to express this new reality.

Abstract Painting

Kandinsky [67, 68, 126]

Abstract painting belongs to this formalized view of the world, with its non-visual tendencies, this newly discovered and ever-widening reality; it is its artistic complement and its equal as an expression of man's artistic creativity, and it was no accident that it emerged at the same period.

And it is a pertinent, important detail that Kandinsky, the first artist who risked the decisive step towards complete abstraction, was not able to commit himself to it until he had become aware that material was changing into energy, until, that is, he ceased to regard the banishment of objectivity from the sphere of painting as a brutal assault.

Thus abstract painting emerged as a contemporary form of the image of reality – and it was born simultaneously in various places, a fact which shows quite clearly once again that this form of painting was closely bound up with the outlook of the new century. Kandinsky ventured on the first abstract picture in 1910. This was the first time that a picture was created which had no basis in perceivable reality. Kandinsky's art derived from German Expressionism: in the *Blaue Reiter* group his work, like the others', had been dominated by colour. His first abstract pictures too were mainly carried by their brilliancy; the drawing, or line, was subordinated to this passionate, excited colour-movement. Curves and patches, together with the colours, created a richly moving, boisterous music, reminiscent of the sound of a large orchestra capable of every musical nuance. The character of these pictures, their content and intellectual message, remains clearly Expressionistic, ecstatic in their whole attitude.

Kupka [69] and Malewitsch [72, 73]

But this abstract language also developed from another starting point: from the strict, clear and formalized grammar of Cubism. In Paris in 1913 the Czech artist Frank Kupka passed from Cubism to abstract compositions notable for their architectonic character and strong feeling for space. In Russia at the same period Kasimir Malewitsch, who had previously been under the influence of French Cubism, discovered his own form of abstract painting: he called it Suprematism. The vocabulary of forms of this painting is restricted exclusively to geometrical forms and bright, unbroken colours. To Malewitsch, Suprematism (whose manifesto he painted in his picture *Black Square on a White Background*) was synonymous with the ascendancy of pure feeling.

The 'De Stijl' Group

The *De Stijl* group was formed in Holland in 1917. It built up and deepened this language of geometrically based abstraction both systematically and ideologically. The vocabulary of pictorial means to which this group (van Doesburg [74], Mondriaan [76, 122], van der Leck [75], Huszar, etc) rigorously restricted itself consisted of the straight line and the right-angle – in other words, horizontals and verticals – the three primary colours, red, yellow and blue, and the three primary non-colours, black, grey and white. With these means the group aimed to give expression to the laws of universal harmony whose portrayal demands an abstract language because they are above both the artist's subjective feeling and the chance objectivity of a detail from nature. As legitimate successors to the iconoclasts these painters banished all objective form from their pictures, so that only absolute harmony should be the content of their painting. These pictures were to lead us to a sight, and thus to a realization of the harmony which had not yet been attained in daily life, although it had already been depicted in paint. Painting as the guide to a new view of the world – that was the magnificent vision that the *De Stijl* painters realized in their work. In the balance of straight lines and pure colours we see the extreme development of an outlook that had left perception behind and was looking for the essence of reality in a visual form.

The First World War

However, this high-toned, indeed utopian, conception of painting and reality did not fail to produce a reaction: the First World War abruptly halted the quest for harmony in this world and made all attempts to create an art attuned to such an outlook appear questionable. With all its cruelty and unimaginable episodes, war produced an outlook which no longer aimed to lay bare the meaning of reality since it sprang from the very meaninglessness, the doubtfulness of reality. Despair, the feeling that all man's work was unavailing, found expression in pictures which, like Odilon Redon's work, belonged to the halfway state between dream and reality.

Chagall [63, 64]

Chagall had rediscovered this world even before the outbreak of war. In his pictures, which grow out of the folklore of the Russian Jews, we experience things which we have previously met only in fairy tales – men who fly through the air, animals and men in familiar conversation, villages which drift down from heaven... This attachment to the world of dreams and fables makes the improbable seem real in Chagall's pictures, and the fantastic believable. An optimistic warmth radiates from his works and fills the half-dream world with a moving, poetic magic.

Italy: de Chirico [80]

But not all the pictures that grow out of this dream-world bear the marks of *joie de vivre*. At first in Italy, in the middle of the First World War, they had the feeling of nightmare. A number of Italian artists who returned from the war (chief among them being de Chirico) started by translating the feeling of uncertainty, the puzzling quality òf things, into visual forms. These works (*pittura metafisica*) show objects stranded in oppressive and empty space, so that, looking at them, we are seized by a feeling of panic anxiety – an anxiety which derives not only from these abandoned, strange objects and the silence surrounding them, but equally from the hard, plastically suggestive style of painting: it is as though one would be bound to collide with each of these things – they are strange, but also unavoidable.

The meaninglessness of reality – obvious in war – is reflected in the strangeness and unconnected feeling of these inanimate objects.

Dada

In 1916 a group of artists was formed in Switzerland who went even further in emphasizing, indeed denouncing, the senselessness of reality. By way of declaring their attitude they took the meaningless name 'Dada'. Duchamp [52], Ernst [88] and Picabia [83] belonged to the group, and Schwitters [77] soon joined it. They satirized reality, arbitrarily raising certain things to the level of 'art' by selecting them for exposure. They created pictures by mixing the most arbitrarily chosen objects – in short, in all their pictures they demonstrated that chance is more meaningful than reality and more rational than the human mind.

Surrealism

Surrealism, the current of European painting which left its stamp on the whole period between the wars, flowed from these two sources, Dada and metaphysical painting. It emerged as an artistic trend in 1923–4, out of the attempt (violently opposed by the Dadaists) to find a system for the type of painting which had taken so many forms and pictures from the halfway state between dreams and reality. This very systemization seemed to the Dadaists to be the direst threat to their view of the world; for the meaninglessness, chance, anarchy of this world brooked no method – and any system was bound to be either hypocrisy or betrayal.

Nevertheless a number of artists – poets and painters – made an attempt at systemization and indeed succeeded in laying down a scientific basis for *aperçus* that had been discovered in the painter's practical work. In their contact with Sigmund Freud, the father of psychoanalysis, they discovered the analogy between artistic and psychological rules and functions. So from the very beginning Surrealism appears not as a trend of painting but as a human way of dealing with reality, a form of awareness of reality and oneself. In this type of artistic philosophy the organization of the mind, the rule of the reason, are excluded from the creative process: pictures and ideas emerge in a strange way out of the depths of the unconscious, and the result (as well as the aim) of the Surrealists' work is to make visible this strangeness and oddity which they see as the truest reality. So it is understandable that Surrealism, which never was or aimed to be an artistic style, shows no artistic unity in its works; side by side, corresponding to the two sources of the stream, we find hard, objective paintings and fantastic abstractions which have nothing in common but the process which gives birth to the picture–this mysterious emergence of a vision from the unconscious mind.

Magritte [87], Delvaux [86], Dali [85] and Tanguy [84]

The objective, highly detailed Surrealist painting found its firmest foothold in Belgium (Magritte and Delvaux), although in France too it gained an adherent, Yves Tanguy, the most articulate exponent of this trend, along with Dali, from Spain, whose equal he is. The painting technique of these Surrealist artists is as precise as the old masters', and sometimes painfully hard – they vie with photography in trying to reproduce details faithfully. But the objects which are portrayed with such fidelity to perception come from a completely strange reality: they are objects which one would never meet in real life, and with which only the imagination could bring one into contact in the freest of free associations. And it is from this great fidelity to detail, this almost photographic precision in the reproduction of such strange encounters that the shock of this miraculous quality (which is what the Surrealists are aiming at) is derived.

Joan Mirò [112]

But within the Surrealist trend there are, of course, other painters who reject this fidelity to outward appearance. To them this kind of fantastic combination of fragments of reality is still too much of a compromise with meaningless, inessential reality. Their form of painting is automatic writing – the complete elimination of the controlling intelligence, pictures transferred direct from the subconscious to the canvas by way of the hand. Man – the artist – thus becomes the seismograph of a union existing between nature and man: he draws the subterranean stirrings, the convulsions and rifts deep within which perception cannot see but which man, as a sensitive instrument, can feel.

Joan Mirò is the master of this school, and his fantastically mobile pictures, made up of tangled linear movement and glowing colours, translate something of the miracle of this newly discovered reality into a pictorial language. The magic of this new reality resides precisely in the fact that it can never be completely captured in words, pictures or ideas.

Ernst [88] and Schwitters [77]

Two painters found their own paths out of this world of the absurd and fantastic – Max Ernst and Kurt Schwitters. Both were originally connected with the Dada group, from whose view of life their pictorial vision sprang. Max Ernst was concerned to reveal and conjure up the inner rhythm, often hostile and malignant, of nature; to attain this he often made use of chance patterns created by nature – the grain of wood, cloud-formations – and by concentrating his gaze on these structures he called up visions which convey an idea of the ambiguity and treacherousness of reality. This has produced pictures of great suggestive power. Schwitters started out from chance material in a different way: he collected litter – tram tickets, rags, brown paper, etc – and assembled these finds into a new composition suggested by the material itself. Things which man has thrown away and cast off, which appear meaningless, nevertheless combine to form a new magical organization, a special reality, if one knows how to perceive their essence.

Sunday Painters and 'die Neue Sachlichkeit'

The shock and disillusionment which were consequences of the First World War and which gave rise to the nightmare world of Surrealism, shook all faith in a meaningful reality and allowed a faith in the miraculous to break through. Surrealism had discovered the miraculous and conjured it up in the halfway kingdom between waking and dreaming. A number of artists – some of them not professional painters – rediscovered this miraculous quality in everyday reality; these were the Sunday painters, artists with a naïve vision of reality, and the *Neue Sachlichkeit* painters. In a world whose meaning seemed to have disappeared, and where the relationship between things was no longer comprehensible, everyday, commonplace reality seemed the greatest miracle of all: here at least life went on undisturbed and undisrupted, as it had done for so long. But only a person who was in the midst of this world, for whom its reality had never become a problem, could paint it in this way. Thus these Sunday painters – countrymen, postmen, a charwoman – painted their world of unproblematical reality with naïve eyes, in France [108, 109, 115], Yugoslavia [114] and Haiti; and all the others, for whom the world *had* become a problem, found a new wonder, paradise regained, in this naïve view of the world. It is not so much the recrudescence of this almost timeless folk-art, as the way it was enthusiastically accepted into the art-world, which is a typical phenomenon of this century. This yearning for an existence without problems, for an assured reality, is evinced again in the *Neue Sachlichkeit* painting. With an almost religious devotion, a kind of *devotio moderna*, these painters (Dix [116], Spencer [117], Charley Toorop [118]) depict the objects of everyday life in all their ugliness as samples from a reality not yet corroded by the decay of our view of the world.

The Bauhaus

Feininger [71], Kandinsky [67, 68, 126], Klee [65, 66, 144] and Schlemmer [70]

But in the years between the wars the opposite pole to this romantic yearning, reflected both in the Surrealists' pictures and in those of the naïve and the *Neue Sachlichkeit* painters, was a strict architectonic discipline, a mental drill whose spiritual home was the Bauhaus, first in Weimar, later in Dessau. The aim of this community of artists was to erect the building of the future in which all the arts should play their part. Like the mediaeval cathedral, it was to be a symbol of the contemporary view of the world. Artists of every kind were to be trained at the Bauhaus, from disciplined craftsmen to creative artists, and in this development the fine arts were to have a place as a laboratory, a field for free investigation. The first leading figure of the Bauhaus, Walter Gropius the architect, had the discernment to summon four of the great artists of the time for this task – Feininger, Kandinsky, Klee and Schlemmer. So in the small Bauhaus circle the spirit of the *Blaue Reiter* (inspired by Kandinsky and Klee) and the strict pictorial discipline of Feininger and Schlemmer, trained on Cubism, mingled in fruitful cooperation. From the *Blaue Reiter* came the humble readiness to pay attention to the laws of nature and give them precedence over personal inspiration; whereas the austere pictorial structure, in an architectural mode, of the two other artists shows clearly that Cubist, and hence Cézanne's, doctrines lived on in them. In the Bauhaus a view of the world which held the balance between feeling and reason seemed to take shape for the first time – and herein lies the reason for both the magnificent effect and the vulnerability of this experiment, which is still an example to many artists today.

It is the very multiplicity of the trends pursued by the four artists who worked together in such great intimacy in the Bauhaus that made this co-operation so fruitful and abundant. Because of his contact with the Russian Constructivists during his stay in Russia in the war years, Kandinsky, the oldest, had arrived at a clearer, more precise style. The forcefulness of his first abstract compositions had given way to more of a chamber music-like transparency, while the imaginative intellectuality which had characterized his work in the *Blaue Reiter* period remained as strong as ever.

It was not until he was summoned to the Bauhaus that Paul Klee revealed the true richness of his creative personality; in his small, exquisite oil paintings and water-colours he devised forms following the rules of nature, played variations on themes given him by nature and, with his impressive imagination, achieved results which created a new, unsuspected reality and made it credible. By humbly observing reality and, of course, carefully weighing his pictorial means Klee managed to distil the essence from objects, their less precise associations largely free from their precise forms. To do this he evolved a style akin to Egyptian hieroglyphics.

Feininger, whose contribution to the Bauhaus's production is at the opposite pole to Klee's, presents the spirit of architecture as the dominant factor in his work. His pictures – old towns, towers, churches – soar up before our eyes like crystals, clearly constructed and transparent. The laws of architecture also govern space and atmosphere, so that the air-space round the buildings in his pictures is constructed out of the same architectonic material as the buildings: in Feininger's work the architect's art and discipline enter into painting.

And in both his paintings and his stage designs Schlemmer, the youngest of the four, tries to bring this architecture into harmony with man's image, so that man inspires it, gives it tension and life. In Schlemmer's work we see a splendid rebirth of Seurat's attempt to transform all reality into a contrapuntal composition. From these four artists and the atmosphere they created at the Bauhaus there emerged, clearly and splendidly, a view of the world in which the human mind and its discipline were appointed architects of reality.

Between the Two World Wars

Beckmann [100, 168], Soutine [42], van den Berghe [92] and Makovski [107]

Between the wars painting swung between these two poles – on the one hand, a yearning for the miraculous, for the non-rational, the revealing, and on the other, the urge to create a new reality according to intellectual laws wrested from nature. The influence of Surrealism could be felt almost everywhere, even in Picasso's work, and if a great painter like Max Beckmann seems to have escaped its influence this is merely because he portrayed the oppression and *Weltangst* expressed in Surrealism in a different way, with Expressionistic means, in his work. The point of departure of his painting was the hardness of reality, its ruthlessness, against which man has to struggle. Thus a picture becomes a drama and consequently demands Expressionistic means – contrast, dramatically taut space, the theatrical attitude of the figure. In general, though Expressionism went through a new Golden Age in the years between the wars, nevertheless it adopted many elements of Surrealism, anxiety and *Weltangst* – most clearly in Soutine's feverishly convulsive pictures, but also in the work of the Belgian Expressionists (above all Frits van den Berghe) and the gifted Polish painter, Makovski.

Léger [58, 79, 164], Matisse Campigli, [82], Morandi [81] and Rivera [101]
One can sense a similar influence, not perhaps of Surrealism itself but
rather of the attitude to life expressed in Surrealism, in the work of
those artists who, following Cézanne and the Cubists, depicted reality
according to the strict rules of geometry and pictorial syntax. But they
were chiefly aiming to subordinate the pictorial entity to the laws of
architecture, rather like the Bauhaus artists. Léger's astringent pictures,
painted in the twenties, are a pointed example of how the strict lan-
guage-discipline of Cubism found its way to the similar strictness of the
new architecture which was indeed largely inspired by the principles of
the *De Stijl* group and the Bauhaus. And in Campigli's pictures the trend
towards mural painting is clearly visible, in both the structure of the
composition and the dull colours, approximating to the colours of a
wall – although he worked on canvas and on small canvases too. But
it was above all the great Mexican school of painting, Rivera, Orozco
[120] and Siqueiros [121], who succeeded in this quest for the mural and
gave it historical actuality.

This attempt to produce pictures which would be the anonymous
expression of a human order and would embody all human attempts
to realize an architectonic view of the world, an idea which had possessed
many artists since Seurat, came to life again and became topical shortly
before the outbreak of the Second World War. Artists such as Léger,
Matisse, Campigli and Morandi worked on this and, in doing so, gave
expression to a hope of mankind.

After the Second World War

The Second World War interrupted this development. For five years
silence was imposed on painting in Europe (and elsewhere) by an
inhumanity and wild barbarism inimical to all art. A few artists had had
presentiments of this: Picasso's *Guernica*, painted in 1937 after one of
the first occasions when unarmed men were murdered (which was
followed by many similar, much more horrible outrages) was a warning,
a 'writing on the wall', whose meaning was little appreciated.

Painting as it emerged in 1944–5 after the years of horror and silence
bore a different appearance from pre-war painting. Many of the painters
of the pre-war period had not survived the war: Kandinsky, Klee and
Mondriaan had died before the end of the nightmare. And afterwards
those who did survive found a world whose wishes and cares were
different from their own: so their work is a splendid completion of a
period behind us, a late harvesting of a past summer, rather than a
direct contribution to the view of the world of the post-war years. Old

themes crop up again: Léger's robust optimism in his mural-like compositions [164], the inexorable drama in Beckmann's late triptychs, the classic restraint and economy of means in the collages which represent a high-point in Matisse's work [165]. In his latest pictures, whose theme is the artist's studio, Braque has attained a freedom which does not conflict with his strict discipline, and Picasso, the most many-sided and also the most intense painter of his generation, frequently turns to the art of earlier masters, playing his own completely contemporary variations on them [169], improvising on them with sovereign skill.

The New Generation

But the period after the war really belongs to a new generation and a new view of the world. Of the pre-war artists Kandinsky and Mondriaan, and later Klee, were felt to be trend-setters, for the language for everything this new generation had to say was abstract painting. This was a young generation which had had to stifle all hopes of a better, brighter world during the war – and after the war found all these hopes destroyed and confounded by events. A generation, that is, in something like the situation of the Romantics at the beginning of the nineteenth century. Views of reality, philosophies of life had become minor affairs; the question was whether one could live in this world at all. So the quest for a view of the world was replaced with an attempt to express a new feeling for life; they were more concerned with what went on in men confronted with reality than with conveying a valid picture of reality itself.

Action Painting: Pollock [143] and de Kooning [150]

The generation of artists who took the stage after the war prized deeds above knowledge, belief in life above perspicacity: this explains the emergence in the United States of action painting, in which the painter puts the rhythms of his own movement on to the canvas in an ecstatic dance. Incidentally, this form of painting has much in common with another contemporary art-form – jazz. There too the artist does not start out from a previously determined plan but gives free rein to the stream of his consciousness and his temperament. Jackson Pollock and Willem de Kooning are the pioneers of this ecstatic painting, with its Dionysian impulse, in America; with its wild excitement, it also abandoned the traditional means of painting – the brush and palette.

The Cobra Group: Jorn [162], Alechinsky and Appel [163]

At almost the same time as the American group, a European group of similar outlook was formed out of painters from Copenhagen, Brussels and Amsterdam (the Co-Br-A group). Its leading spirit was Asger Jorn a Dane, and others involved were Alechinsky, Appel, Constant and Corneille [145]. The world of these men's pictures is a fiery, harsh protest against all outward order, against aestheticism and optimism – a loud, shrill summons to spontaneity and honesty. Forms and colours, pictorial images, stream from an uncontrolled, frenzied imagination to become communication on the canvas – to let us participate in the artist's experience.

This shift of emphasis from the picture of reality to the demonstration of a feeling about life took place in Europe and America in the years immediately after the end of the war as a new generation came to the attack. While in both Europe and America older painters worked to develop Kandinsky's and Mondriaan's abstract language still further, to create in it works of a harmonious balance, there were other (usually much younger) painters everywhere who could see only a dishonest extenuation in this harmony and who wanted to shout forth their protest, disgust and disillusionment – but also their yearning for honesty and truth. It is true of them all that they allow themselves to be guided not by thought-out pictorial ideas but only by improvisations rising within them and bursting from them.

Fautrier [146], Dubuffet [151], de Staël [135], Wols [142] and da Silva [166]

Fautrier's pictures springing up out of a thick impasto, Dubuffet's montages of material and his tangled networks of lines (curiously like tree-mosses), Wols's fine spider's-web-like watercolours, tinted with ink-like colours, as well as Hartung's [141] bundles of lines, painted with violent dynamism, de Staël's intertwined patches of colour and Vieira da Silva's interlaced rods overcome with fear of space – all these spring from the feeling for life of artists who no longer give themselves up trustingly to constructive work on a picture of reality, but grasp fiercely and abruptly at the teachings of instinct, vitality, a physical feeling for life; or let themselves be stimulated by what the material suggests so that the primitive forces of nature may be evoked by the retention of 'primitive' materials, such as rusty iron plates, etc, in the finished work of art.

The Problem Remains the Same

At this present stage of contemporary painting the pictures of the most gifted painters of the younger generation suggest that the distinction between abstract and figurative painting is on the decline. For the feeling of the post-war years, the urge towards honest and direct communication with his fellow-men, has made the artist grasp first at the one means of communication, then at the other. The essential and significant point is above all the way in which this painting expresses the general outlook of the world of our age: through the subjective expression which the artist now and then heightens to the pitch of a mystical experience. In this the painting of the post-war era has remained faithful to the *leitmotiv* of the whole century: like Paul Klee's work, it attempts not to reproduce the visible but to make things visible. And so it is a link in a chain which began almost a hundred years ago and will stretch through the present into the future – a chain of pictures of which only a few are reproduced in this book to illustrate the course of development, the various phases of artists' concern with the problem.

For the problem remains the same. It is the question men have been asking themselves throughout this century and wrestling with not only in the sphere of painting, but in literature, philosophy, science and history – the question of the essence of reality and the place man occupies in it. The answer humanity will give to this question will not only be expressed in painting; for it will decide and determine the fate of humanity itself, and with it painting too. And in our century this answer will be given by humanity as a whole – not one country or one city, as in the past; art too has become the property of all mankind and now is the time for all of us to listen to the message the painting of our age brings and will continue to bring us.

Twentieth-Century Painting

Illustrations

1 Paul Cézanne

2 Paul Cézanne

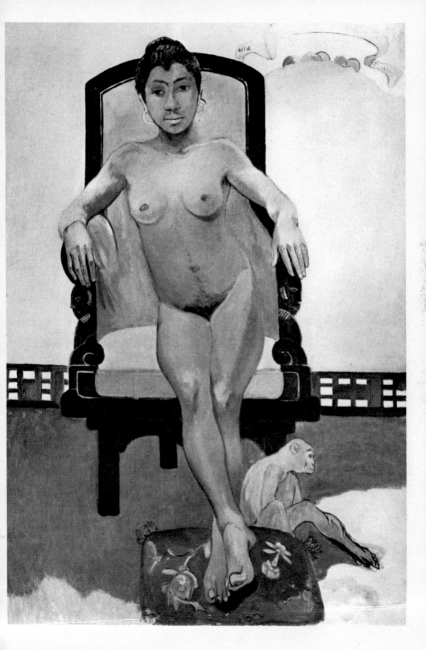

3　Paul Gauguin

4 Paul Gauguin

5   Vincent van Gogh

6 Vincent van Gogh

7 Vincent van Gogh

8 Georges Seurat

9 Claude Monet

10 Paul Signac

11　Pierre Bonnard

12 Pierre Bonnard

13 Edouard Vuillard

14   Edouard Vuillard

15 Ker Xavier Roussel

16   Odilon Redon

17   James Ensor

18 Maurice Denis

19   Félix Vallotton

20 Henri Rousseau

21　Pablo Picasso

22 Rik Wouters

23   Walter Richard Sickert

24   Maurice Utrillo

25 Amedeo Modigliani

26 Paula Modersohn-Becker

27 Lovis Corinth

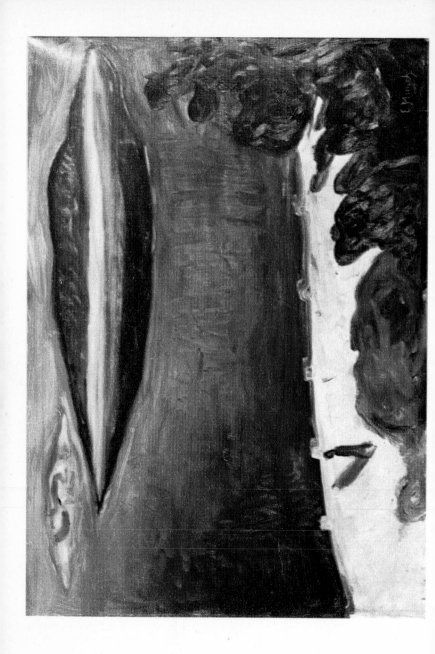

28 Edvard Munch

29 Pierre Bonnard

30 Ferdinand Hodler

31 Albert Marquet

32   Henri Matisse

83　Henri Matisse

34 Maurice de Vlaminck

35   André Derain

36 Erich Heckel

37   Karl Schmidt-Rottluff

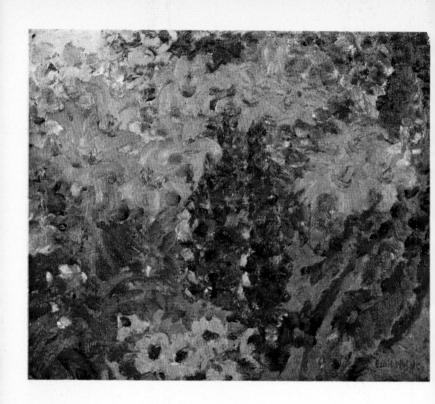

38   Emil Nolde

39   Ernst Ludwig Kirchner

40   Raoul Dufy

41 Alexej von Jawlensky

42   Chaim Soutine

43 Georges Rouault

44　Oskar Kokoschka

45   Kees van Dongen

46   Pablo Picasso

47 Georges Braque

48 Pablo Picasso

49   Georges Braque

50   Roger de la Fresnaye

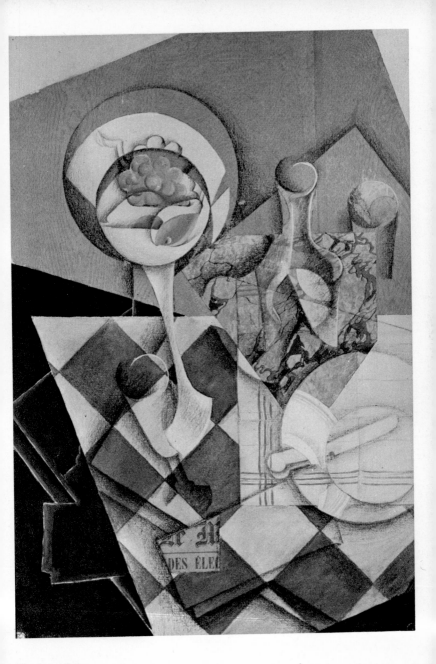

51 Juan Gris

52 Marcel Duchamp

54 Carlo Carrà

56 Jacques Villon

57 Michail Larionoff

58 Fernand Léger

59 Robert Delaunay

60 August Macke

61 Heinrich Campendonk

62 Franz Marc

63 Marc Chagall

64   Marc Chagall

65 Paul Klee

66 Paul Klee

67 Wassilij Kandinsky

68   Wassilij Kandinsky

69 Frank Kupka

70 Oskar Schlemmer

71 Lyonel Feininger

72 Kasimir Malewitsch

73 Kasimir Malewitsch

74 Theo van Doesburg

75 Bart van der Leck

76 Piet Mondriaan

77 Kurt Schwitters

78   El Lissitzky

79   Fernand Léger

82   Massimo Campigli

83 Francis Picabia

84 Yves Tanguy

85　Salvador Dali

86 Paul Delvaux

87 René Magritte

88   Max Ernst

89   Ben Shahn

90   Jean Lurçat

91 Lasar Segall

92 Frits van den Berghe

93   Constant Permeke

94   André Dunoyer de Segonzac

95 Raymond-Jean Legueult

96 René Auberjonois

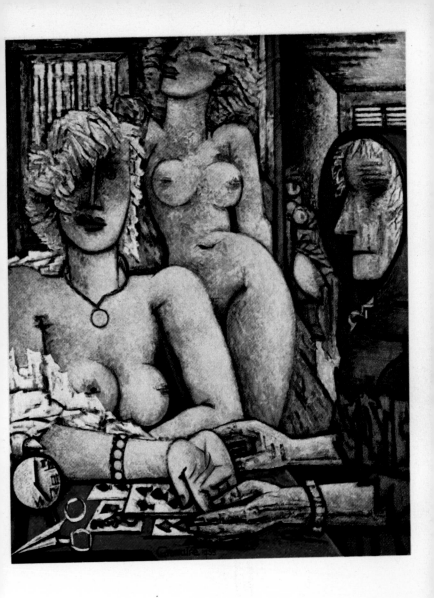

97 Marcel Gromaire

98   John Marin

99 Georgia O'Keeffe

100 Max Beckmann

101   Diego Rivera

102 Christian Gaillard

103 Christian Rohlfs

104 - 105   Pablo Picasso

106 Vaclav Spala

107   Tadeusz Makovski

108 Séraphine

109 Camille Bombois

110 Herman Kruyder

111 Jean Brusselmans

112   Joan Miró

113   André Marchand

114   Ivan Generalič

115   André Bauchant

116 Otto Dix

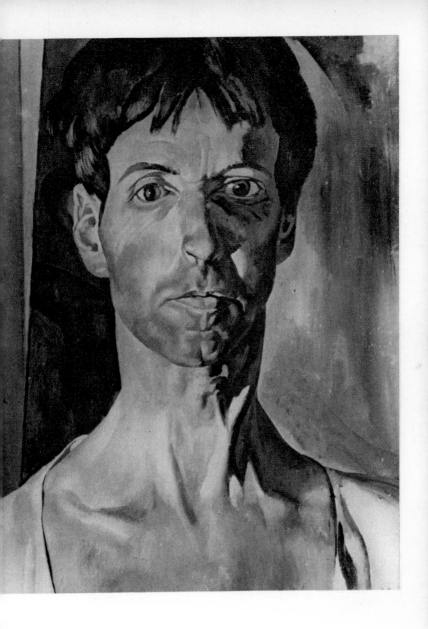

17   Stanley Spencer

118 Charley Toorop

119 Renato Guttuso

120 José Clemente Orozco

121 David Alfaro Siqueiros

122 Piet Mondriaan

123 César Domela

124　Richard Mortensen

125 Victor Vasarely

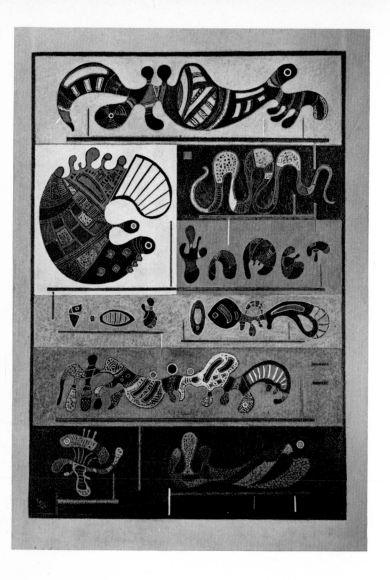

127 Alberto Magnelli

128　Georges Braque

129   Petar Lubarda

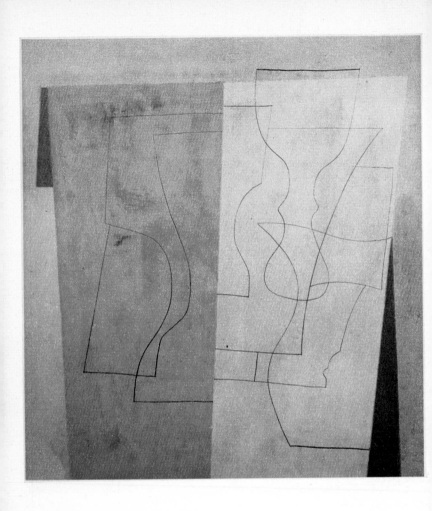

130   Ben Nicholson

31 Willi Baumeister

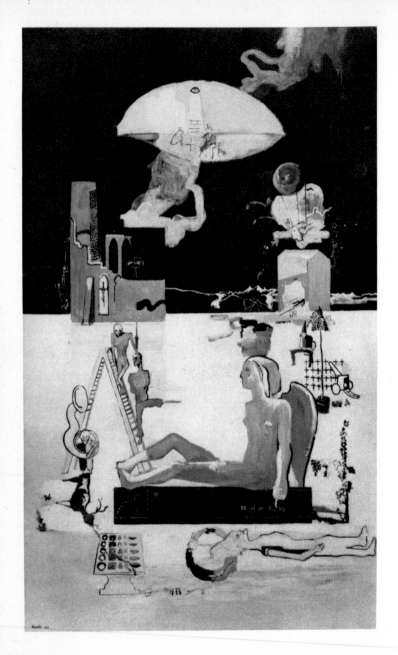

132 Walter Kurt Wiemken

133 Gerrit Benner

134   Ernst Wilhelm Nay

135   Nicolas de Staël

7　Alfred Manessier

138 Jean Bazaine

139 Roger Bissière

140 Fritz Winter

141 Hans Hartung

142   Wols

43　Jackson Pollock

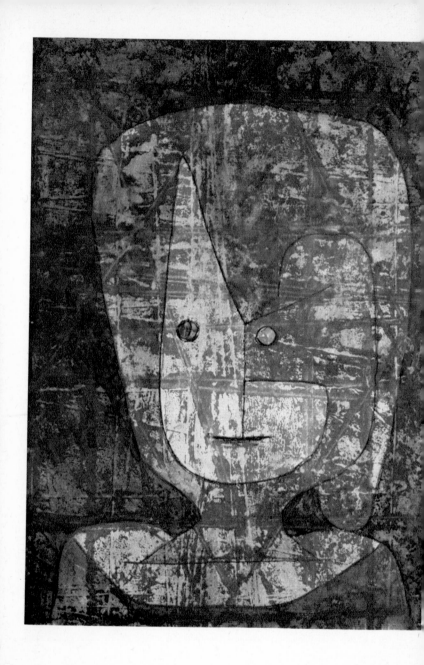

144 Paul Klee

145   Corneille

146 Jean Fautrier

47 Emil Schumacher

148   Pierre Soulages

49 Franz Kline

150 Willem de Kooning

151 Jean Dubuffet

152 Bernard Buffet

153 Francis Bacon

154 Graham Sutherland

156   Wifredo Lam

157 Roberto E.Matta

158   Arshile Gorky

159   Joseph Zaritsky

160 Paul-Emil Borduas

161 Jean-Paul Riopelle

162 Asger Jorn

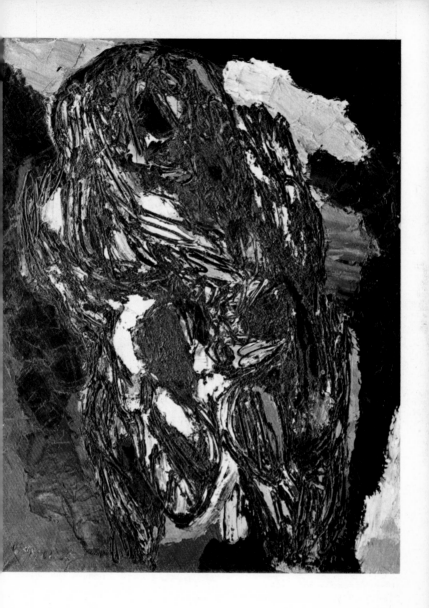

163 Karel Appel

164   Fernand Léger

165 Henri Matisse

166 Maria Elena Vieira da Silva

167　Mark Tobey

168 Max Beckmann

169   Pablo Picasso

170 Bram van Velde

171 Serge Poliakoff

172 Jaap Wagemaker

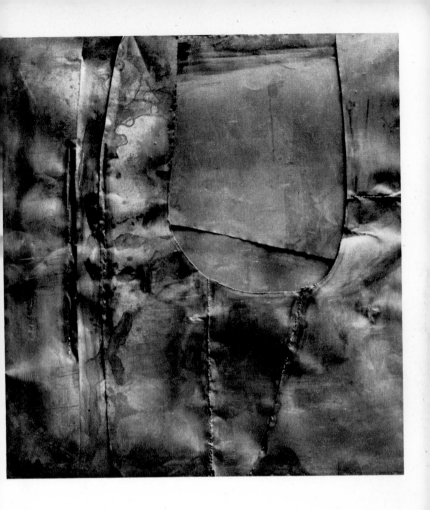

173   Alberto Burri

174 Antonio Tapies

175 Mark Rothko

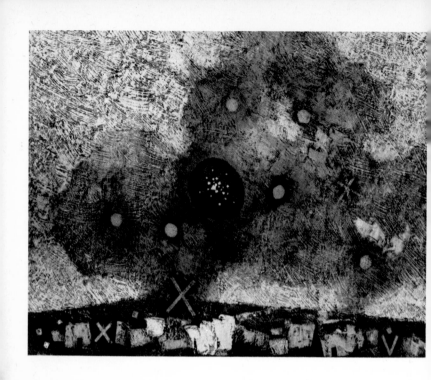

176　Mordechai Ardon

Biographical Notes

The figures in italics in the text refer to the illustrations

Afro (A. Basaldella). Italian painter. Born in Udine in 1912. He was a Cubist for a period and since 1945 has been an important exponent of abstract art in Italy (*fig. 136*)

Appel, Karel. Dutch painter. Born in Amsterdam in 1921. An important exponent of Abstract Expressionism. Co-founder, with Jorn and Corneille, of the Cobra group. Lives in Paris (*fig. 163*)

Ardon, Mordechai. Israeli painter. Born in Tuchow in 1896. Studied at the Bauhaus in Weimar. Has developed an Expressionist style with an individual use of colour and lyrical accents. Lives in Israel (*fig. 176*)

Auberjonois, René. Swiss painter. Born in Yverdon in 1872, died in Lausanne in 1957. An important artist with his own expressive style which he developed after being influenced by Post-Impressionists, Fauves and Cubists (*fig. 96*)

Bacon, Francis. English painter. Born in Dublin in 1909. A self-taught Surrealist. Works in London (*fig. 153*)

Ballà, Giacomo. Italian painter. Born in Turin in 1871, died in Rome in 1958. A leading Futurist who tried to reproduce movement in his works (*fig. 55*)

Bauchant, André. French painter. Born in Château-Renault in 1873, and died in 1958. Worked as a gardener and surveyor and only later began to draw. Was discovered as a painter in 1920. His flower-paintings are idyllically beautiful (*fig. 115*)

Baumeister, Willi. German painter. Born in Stuttgart in 1889, died there in 1955. Important Abstract painter and Constructivist; the aim of his work is to apply architectonic organization to his pictures (*fig. 131*)

Bazaine, Jean. French painter. Born in Paris in 1904. An Abstract artist, he uses harmonious colours and forms which nevertheless always retain a link with nature (*fig. 138*)

Beckmann, Max. German. Produced paintings and drawings. Born in Leipzig in 1884, died in New York in 1950. An Expressionist artist with an individual style characterized by symbols and mythological themes. A master of horrifying allegory (*figs. 100, 168*)

Benner, Gerrit. Dutch painter. Born in Leeuwarden in 1897. Self-taught. Developed his style in the years following the war and with his colours achieved a peaceful expressive quality (*fig. 133*)

Berghe, Frits van den. Belgian painter. Born in Ghent in 1883, died there in 1939. One of the main figures of Flemish Expressionism; in his later work he gave freer rein to his imagination and his art approached Surrealism (*fig. 92*)

Bissière, Roger. French painter. Born in Villeréal in 1888. After a Cubist period, became one of the leading exponents of Abstract art; led a number of significant younger painters towards Abstract painting influenced by Klee (*fig. 139*)

Boccioni, Umberto. Italian painter. Born in Reggio Calabria in 1882, died in Verona on the North Italian Front in 1916. He was the theorist and strongest personality of Futurism (*fig. 53*)

Bombois, Camille. French painter. Born in Venarey-les-Laumes in 1883. At first he painted only as an amateur. It was not until 1922 that he was discovered as a 'naïve painter' in an open-air exhibition. Since then he has devoted himself exclusively to painting. Lives in Paris (*fig. 109*)

Bonnard, Pierre. French painter. Born in Fontenay-aux-Roses in 1867, died in Le Cannet in 1947. A Post-Impressionist painter; he belonged to the group who called themselves the Nabis. He and his friend Vuillard were masters of an intimate type of painting. Bonnard was also a masterly graphic artist, as several famous books illustrated by him bear witness (*figs. 11, 12, 29*)

Borduas, Paul-Emil. Canadian painter. Born in Quebec in 1905, died in Paris in 1960. Borduas was Canada's first Abstract painter: founded the Automation group with Riopelle in 1940 (*fig. 160*)

Braque, Georges. French painter. Born in Argenteuil in 1882. In 1900 he went to Paris, where he joined the Fauves. He became friendly with Othon Friesz. Impressed by Cézanne's painting, which he saw at his memorial exhibition in 1907, he looked for a structural form and, with Picasso, developed Cubism. In 1917 he returned to a more objective, lighter style. In 1930 his style changed again and he created classical harmonies with lines, forms and colours (*figs. 47, 49, 128*)

Brusselmans, Jean. Belgian painter. Born in Brussels in 1884, died in Dilbeek in 1953. In the spirit of Flemish Expressionism Brusselmans developed a robust, monumental style of landscape painting (*fig. 111*)

Buffet, Bernard. French painter. Born in Paris in 1928. Successful figurative artist whose style is based chiefly on graphic effect. Lives in Paris (*fig. 152*)

Burri, Alberto. Italian painter. Born in Citta di Castello in 1915. Abstract painter who uses wood and metal in his collages and montages. Lives in Rome (*fig. 173*)

Campendonk, Heinrich. German. Produced paintings and drawings. Born in Krefeld in 1889, died in 1957 in Amsterdam where he taught at the Academy. Belonged to the *Blaue Reiter* group. Founded a new monumental tradition in Holland (*fig. 61*)

Campigli, Massimo. Italian painter. Born in Florence in 1895. The painting of antiquity is the source of his fresco-like work; his aim is to revive mural painting. Has lived in Paris since 1949 (*fig. 82*)

Carrà, Carlo. Italian painter. Born in Quargnento in 1881. One of the most important figures in modern Italian painting. He, Boccioni and Severini founded Futurism. Like Morandi and de Chirico he turned to 'Metaphysical' painting in 1918, while he later looked towards early Italian painting (Masaccio) (*fig. 54*)

Cézanne, Paul. French painter. Born in Aix-en-Provence in 1839, died there in 1906. In his youth he was a friend of Emile Zola and was influenced by Delacroix and Courbet; later, in Impressionist circles, he was influenced by Pissarro. From 1882 lived mainly in Aix. Here he developed his own style; he traced nature's forms back to si nple, basic geometric forms. Cézanne is one of the direct ancestors of twentieth-century art – above all because of his magnificent attempt to master anew the strict construction of the picture (*figs. 1, 2*)

Chagall, Marc. Russian. Paintings and drawings. Born in Vitebsk in 1887. He blended Fauvist and Cubist influences with the poetry and dream-like quality of the mystical Russian-Jewish world to produce a vision of the greatest importance in modern art (*figs. 63, 64*)

Chirico, Giorgio de. Greek-Italian painter. Born in Volos in 1888. In Paris, from 1911 to 1915, he turned to Cubism; he founded Italian 'Metaphysical' painting, one of the germ cells of Surrealism, but in 1930 he abandoned his Surrealistic lines of development. Lives in Rome (*fig. 80*)

Corinth, Lovis. German painter. Born in East Prussia (Tapiau) in 1858, died in Holland (Zandvoort) in 1925. Studied in Germany, Belgium and Paris. He and Liebermann are the chief exponents of German Impressionism. After 1911 a change took place in his art, which developed an

Expressionistic, loaded quality characterized by strong colours and an excited manner (*fig. 27*)

Corneille (Cornelis van Beverloo). Dutch painter. Born in Liège in 1922. Co-founder of the Cobra group. Works in Paris; his style has matured to become a poetical lyricism (*fig. 145*)

Dali, Salvador. Spanish painter. Born in Figueras in 1904. Highly controversial and much discussed Surrealist figure, influenced by the Italian Metaphysical painters. His style is characterized by the contrast between the almost photographic, exact technique and the irrational visions he chooses to depict (*fig. 85*)

Delaunay, Robert. French painter. Born in Paris in 1885, died in Montpellier in 1941. Pioneer of Abstract art, influenced by the Fauves and Cubists and friendly with the *Blaue Reiter* painters. His experiments, of crucial importance for the future of Abstract art, were chiefly in the sphere of colour (*fig. 59*)

Delvaux, Paul. Belgian painter. Born in Antheit-Lez-Huy, Belgium, in 1897. After seeking a path between Neo-Impressionism and Expressionism he was influenced by de Chirico and his compatriot Magritte and became a leading exponent of the Surrealism of the veristic type (*fig. 86*)

Denis, Maurice. French painter. Born in Grandville in 1870, died in Saint-Germain-en-Laye in 1943. Belonged to the Nabis group and was its most important theorist. Influenced by Gauguin and Seurat. Painted large frescoes in which he contributed greatly towards reviving modern religious art, in a markedly traditional style, which contradicts his early avant-garde leanings (*fig. 18*)

Derain, André. French painter. Born in Chatou in 1880, died in Chambourcy in 1954. A friend of Vlaminck and Matisse. Later he was strongly influenced by classical painting; at the beginning of this century he contributed an important share to the Fauvist revolution (*fig. 35*)

Dix, Otto. German. Paintings and drawings. Born in Unteranhausen (Thuringia) in 1891. A *Neue Sachlichkeit* painter, in whose work the influence of early German artists gradually became more perceptible (*fig. 116*)

Doesburg, Theo van. (C. E. M. Küpper). Dutch painter. Born in Utrecht in 1883, died in Davos in 1931. With his compatriot Mondriaan he was one of the founders of Dutch Abstract art. He worked as a painter and architect and was the theorist and apologist of the new art. He also founded and edited the periodical *De Stijl* which was of enormous importance to the development of modern art. (*fig. 74*)

Domela, César. Dutch painter. Born in Amsterdam in 1900. After beginning with a greatly simplified manner he joined the *Stijl* group in 1924. In 1928 he introduced the third dimension into his compositions, and the contrast between various materials played an important part in this. Lives in Paris (*fig. 123*)

Dongen, Kees van (Cornelius van). Dutch painter. Born in Delfshaven in 1877. At the age of twenty he went to Paris, where he was influenced by the Impressionists. Later he adopted the Expressionist style of the Fauves and became a member of the *Brücke* group. For a fairly long time he was a favourite society portraitist, but in all his works he remained an outstanding colourist. Lives in Paris (*fig. 45*)

Dubuffet, Jean. French painter. Born in 1901. An exponent of 'informal art', his work stems from the relationship between the structure of natural materials (leaves, sand, etc) and the forms of the subconscious (*fig. 151*)

Duchamp, Marcel. French painter. Born in Blainville in 1887. With his picture *Nu descendant un escalier* (exhibited in 1912) he became well known as a Futurist. In New York he became friendly with Francis Picabia, with whom he founded the American Dada movement. He invented the 'ready-made' – in which mechanical objects are ironically raised to the status of works of art (*fig. 52*)

Dufy, Raoul. French painter. Born in Le Havre in 1877, died in Forcalquier in 1953. In 1900 he went to Paris where he moved in artistic circles and was influenced by the Fauves and, primarily, Matisse. With his light and playful style he developed into one of the most popular French painters of the first half of this century (*fig. 40*)

Dunoyer de Segonzac, André. French painter. Born in Boussy-Saint-Antoine, in 1884. Best known modern landscape painter, influenced by the Impressionists and Cubists. Outstanding graphic artist (*fig. 94*)

Ensor, James. Belgian painter and etcher. Born in Ostend in 1860, died there in 1949. In his work – often pictures showing masked men and skeletons – there appear for the first time the signs of a *Weltangst* which was to find expression in the Surrealism of the twentieth century. Ensor was the greatest predecessor of Surrealism (*fig. 17*)

Ernst, Max. German-American. Paintings and drawings. Born in Brühl in 1891. One of the first German Dadaists: in 1921 he joined the Surrealists in Paris. Since 1941 he has lived largely in the United States (*fig. 88*)

Fautrier, Jean. French painter. Born in Paris in 1898. Abstract artist who at a very early period explored the possibilities of the suggestive effect of the material and the spontaneous application of colour. He was one of the pioneers of a spontaneous Abstract formal language. Lives near Paris (*fig. 146*)

Feininger, Lyonel. German-American painter. Born in New York in 1871, died there in 1956. Cubist painter with an individual style and pictorial for which is architectonic in flavour and very lively in colour. He belonged to the Bauhaus in Dessau (*fig. 71*)

Gaillard, Christian. Swiss painter. Born in Clichy in 1899. Best known modern representational painter in Switzerland (*fig. 102*)

Gauguin, Paul. French painter and wood-carver. Born in Paris in 1848, died in the Marquesas Islands in 1903. In 1883, after having worked as stockbroker, he devoted himself entirely to painting. In 1887 he stayed in Martinique, and in 1888 he worked with van Gogh for a short period. In 1895 he settled for good in the South Sea islands. In his life with the natives he found a new simple reality for his art. He influenced the development of modern art by discovering a vocabulary of forms which stemmed from the original elements of man's art (*figs. 3, 4*)

Generalič, Ivan. Yugoslav painter. Born in Klebine in 1914. Was self-taught at first and developed his art with the help of Hegedusic. In its themes and forms his painting is peasant art, springing from ancient national sources. Generalič is the leader of the Klebine school (*fig. 114*)

Gogh, Vincent van. Dutch painter. Born in Groot Zundert in 1853, committed suicide in Auvers-sur-Oise in 1890. One of the direct ancestors of modern art. He was mainly self-taught, though influenced by Millet and Israels. In Paris in 1886 his brother Theo introduced him to the Impressionists and Japanese woodcuts, and in this year he came to know Gauguin. In 1888 he went to Arles where he discovered his own style, centred entirely on expression and passion. In this year, after a visit from Gauguin, he had a nervous collapse after which he went into a home. In 1890 he moved to Auvers-sur-Oise where Dr Gachet looked after him. On 27 July of that year he shot himself in the chest and died two days later (*figs. 5–7*)

Gorky, Arshile (pseudonym for Vosdanig Adoian). American painter. Born in Armenia in 1904, committed suicide in New York in 1948. Gorky was a pioneer of Abstract art in America and one of the first American Abstract Expressionists (*fig. 158*)

Gris, Juan (José Victoriano Gonzalès). Spanish-French painter. Born in Madrid in 1887, died in Boulogne-sur-Seine in 1927. He, Picasso and Braque are perhaps the leading exponents of Cubism. He pointed the way out of analytical Cubism, which aimed at analysis of the objects, to synthetic Cubism, through which he aimed to achieve 'a re-statement of the object' (*fig. 51*)

Gromaire, Marcel. French painter. Born in Noyelles-sur-Sambre in 1892. Inclined to Expressionism, he is an artist with great decorative power, which has led him, like Lurçat, to revive mural painting and tapestry (*fig. 97*)

Guttuso, Renato. Italian painter. Born in Bergheria (Palermo) in 1912. Turned to painting in 1931. Although influenced by Cubism and Expressionism, this painter, with his strong social impulses, is one of the most important contemporary representational painters (*fig. 119*)

Hartung, Hans. German-French painter. Born in Leipzig in 1904. Settled in Paris in 1935. Has a completely individual style whose strength lies in the dynamic tension of simple, exciting line (*fig. 141*)

Heckel, Erich. German. Paintings and drawings. Born in Döbeln in 1883. Belonged to the group of artists in Dresden known as *Die Brücke*, and so must be counted one of the leading figures of German Expressionism (*fig. 36*)

Hodler, Ferdinand. Swiss painter. Born in Berne in 1853, died in Geneva in 1918. After beginning as a realist, in 1890 he became a Symbolist of enormous power and thus paved the way for Expressionism. His large compositions played a part in the revival of mural painting (*fig. 30*)

Jawlensky, Alexej von. Russian painter. Born in Kuslowo in 1864, died in Wiesbaden in 1941. Became friendly with Kandinsky, with whom (and Klee and Feininger) he founded the group called *Die Blaue Reiter*. Was influenced by Matisse. With its bright colours Jawlensky's painting is related to Russian folk art and became one of the sources of Expressionism (*fig. 41*)

Jorn, Asger. Danish painter. Born in Vejrun in 1914. Co-founder of the Cobra group. Jorn is undoubtedly the most important exponent of the new Expressionism of the post-war years; his painting links Abstract means with a Nordic outlook on life. (*fig. 162*)

Kandinsky, Wassilij. Russian painter. Born in Moscow in 1866, died near Paris in 1944. Kandinsky was the founder and main exponent of so-called 'absolute' painting, and hence a pioneer of Abstract art. In 1910 he produced the first purely Abstract painting, and so took the decisive step into Abstract art. He was a friend of Jawlensky, Marc and Klee and belonged to the Bauhaus in Dessau (*figs. 67, 68, 126*)

Kirchner, Ernst Ludwig. German. Paintings and drawings. Born in Aschaffenourg in 1880, committed suicide in Davos in 1938. German Expressionist, member of the *Brücke* group in Dresden. A great landscape painter and an important graphic artist. He is the main figure in German Expressionism and remained faithful to the principles of expressive art up to his death (*fig. 39*)

Klee, Paul. Swiss-German. Paintings and drawings. Born in Münchenbuchsee in 1879, died near Locarno in 1940. Created a whole language of symbols and was of the greatest importance to modern art; in fact, he is one of the fathers of modern art. From 1920 to 1930 he belonged to the Bauhaus where he worked with Kandinsky, Feininger and Schlemmer (*figs. 65, 66, 144*)

Kline, Franz. American painter. Born in Wilkes-Barre, Pennsylvania, in 1910, died in New York in 1962. An important figure in American Abstract art and one of the men who invented Action Painting. His large-format black and white drawings probably derive from Eastern calligraphy (*fig. 149*)

Kokoschka, Oskar. Austrian. Paintings and drawings. Born in Pöchlarn in 1886. Began as an illustrator and designer. In 1908 he produced his first Expressionist paintings. With his portraits and landscapes Kokoschka became the chief exponent of dramatic Expressionism. During the war he lived in England, and since then has lived mainly in Switzerland (*fig. 44*)

Kooning, Willem de. American painter. Born in Rotterdam in 1904. An important figure in American Abstract art with Expressionistic tendencies (*fig. 150*)

Kruyder, Herman. Dutch painter. Born in Lage Vuursche in 1881, died in Amsterdam in 1935. One of the most important Dutch Expressionists (*fig. 110*)

Kupka, Frank (František). Czech painter. Born in Opocno in 1871, died near

Paris in 1957. Worked mainly in Paris and is considered one of the first masters of Abstract art; his first Abstract pictures, deriving from Cubism, date from 1910; the strictness of his pictorial architecture makes him a predecessor of geometrical abstraction. (*fig. 69*)

La Fresnaye, Roger de. French painter. Born in Le Mans in 1885, died in Grasse in 1925. An important Cubist who painted with glowing colours. Many still-lifes and landscapes. Influenced by Cézanne and the Nabis (*fig. 50*)

Lam, Wifredo. Cuban painter. Born in Sagna la Grande in 1902. Influenced by Picasso. Surrealist in whose work the magical power of the Latin American cultures becomes important pictorially. Lives in the United States (*fig. 156*)

Larionoff, Michail. Russian painter. Born in Tiraspol in 1881, died in Paris in 1962. Founded 'Rayonism' which was the Russian equivalent of Italy's Futurism and which held rays and patches of colour to be the most important components of painting (*fig. 57*)

Leck, Bart van der. Dutch painter. Born in Utrecht in 1876, died in Blaricum in 1958. An Abstract painter, friend of Mondriaan and contributor to *De Stijl*. Later only applied his Abstract style to three-dimensional work (*fig. 75*)

Léger, Fernand. French painter. Born in Aregentan in 1881, died in Gif-sur-Yvette in 1955. Began as a Cubist and first belonged to the group which assigned an important role to colour and reduced form to simple elements. After 1920 he found his own style of strict objectivity in which objects like monuments, strongly contrasted in form and colour, confront each other. In this his importance and influence on modern art, particularly murals, are considerable (*figs. 58, 79, 164*)

Legueult, Raymond-Jean. French painter and tapestry designer. Born in Paris, 1898 (*fig. 95*)

Lissitzky, El (Lasar). Russian painter. Born in Smolensk in 1890, died in Moscow in 1941. Abstract, Constructivist artist, a friend of Malewitsch.

Wrote *The Isms of Art* in 1925 in collaboration with Arp (*fig. 78*)

Lubarda, Petar. Yugoslav painter. Born in Ljubolenjc in 1905. His style, related to Abstract Expressionism, combines a lively vocabulary of symbols with the strict discipline of mural painting (*fig. 129*)

Lurçat, Jean. French painter and tapestry-designer. Born in Bruyères in 1892. He was the man who above all revived the art of tapestry in the twentieth century. He developed his own expressive and Surrealist style and since 1937, working with the Aubusson tapestry-weavers, has raised it to an individual level of brilliance (*fig. 90*)

Macke, August. German painter. Born in Meschede in 1887, died at Perthes in 1914. One of the most important German painters of his generation. One of the *Blaue Reiter* group. His art reflects the *joie de vivre* of his Rhenish temperament, particularly in its bright, glowing colours (*fig. 60*)

Magnelli, Alberto. Italian painter. Born in Florence in 1888. Self-taught Abstract artist who, after a representational interlude, returned to Abstract art with a strict geometrical tendency in early 1930 (*fig. 127*)

Magritte, René. Belgian painter. Born in Lessines in 1898. Important Surrealist who uses a veristic style to show objects from daily life combined together in absurd conjunctions (*fig. 87*)

Makovski, Tadeusz. Polish painter. Born in Oswieam in 1882, died in Paris in 1932. Began as an Impressionist, but discovered Cubism in Paris in 1908. During the First World War he moved closer to Expressionism. The mature style of his later years is characterized by a strict, but lyrical, simplification of form and colour (*fig. 107*)

Malewitsch, Kasimir. Russian painter. Born in Kiev in 1878, died in Leningrad in 1935. At first he was the most important of the Russian Cubists; then in 1913 he devoted himself to his strict 'Suprematism', of which he was the leading exponent (*figs. 72, 73*)

Manessier, Alfred. French painter. Born in Saint-Ouen in 1911. Important figure in Abstract painting which he has applied to the field of religious art, in particular in his church windows. His pictures are based on religio-mystical themes which he formulates in Abstract language. Lives in Paris (*fig. 137*)

Marc, Franz. German painter. Born in Munich in 1880, fell at Verdun in 1916. In Paris came under the influence of the new art; in 1911, with Kandinsky, he founded the Expressionist group called the *Blaue Reiter*. His animal pictures are a significant step in the direction of expressing painting's new feeling for life (*fig. 62*)

Marchand, André. French. Paintings and drawings. Born in Aix-en-Provence in 1907. Occupies a middle position between Abstract and representational painting (*fig. 113*)

Marin, John. American painter. Born in Rutherford, New Jersey, in 1870, died at Cliffside, New Jersey, in 1953. Was influenced by the Fauves and Cubists and became the main exponent of dramatic Expressionism in the United States (*fig. 98*)

Marquet, Albert. French painter. Born in Bordeaux in 1875, died in Paris 1947. Landscape painter of great importance in the Fauves group; he revived the water-colour in France (*fig. 31*)

Matisse, Henri. French. Paintings and drawings. Born in Le Cateau-Cambrésis in 1869, died in Nice in 1954. Began as an Impressionist but in 1905 became the leader of the Fauves group. In the next fifty years or so Matisse produced an enormous *œuvre*, continuously simplifying and reinvigorating his very personal style. He created a world of his own in rich areas of colour with simple drawing. He also illustrated many books, and produced frescoes and glass paintings. He was one of the most important and influential artists of the twentieth century (*figs. 32, 33, 165*)

Matta, Roberto Echaurren. Chilean painter. Born in Santiago in 1912. He is inspired by the world of science and, as a Surrealist, transforms it into magical signs of an inner unrest (*fig. 157*)

Miró, Joan. Spanish painter. Born in Montroig in 1893. This Surrealist and Abstract master of modern art developed his entirely personal, colourful work under the influence of Kandinsky, Arp and Klee. His work reveals a poetic language of great psychological penetration. (*fig. 112*)

Modersohn-Becker, Paula. German painter. Born in Dresden in 1876, died in Worpswede in 1907. Pioneer of German Expressionism; the influence of Gauguin and Cézanne can be felt in her strong, personal and melancholy work (*fig. 26*)

Modigliani, Amedeo. Italian painter. Born in Leghorn in 1884, died in Paris in 1920. In 1907 he arrived in Paris after studying painting in Florence and Venice. He is considered the leader of the École de Paris. His simple forms suggest that he is first and foremost a draughtsman building on the ancient Italian tradition. His art is a confession of the new *Weltschmerz* (*fig. 25*)

Mondriaan, Piet. Dutch painter. Born in Amersfoort in 1872, died in New York in 1944. In 1917 he and Doesburg founded the periodical *De Stijl*, after he had already, in 1912, taken the first steps in the direction which was to lead him to undisputed supremacy in Abstract painting: his horizontal and vertical lines enclose patches of primary colours and present a picture of universal harmony. In his later works in New York he also banished black from his paintings (*figs. 76, 122*)

Monet, Claude. French painter. Born in Paris in 1840, died in Giverny in 1926. Belongs to the Impressionist school and is its most characteristic leading figure. At first he was influenced by Courbet and Jongkind, while he was also impressed by Turner when he visited London in 1870. He was friendly with Pissarro, Renoir and Sisley. His later style, with its atmospheric reflections, makes him a precursor of Abstract painting (*fig. 9*)

Morandi, Giorgio. Italian. Paintings and drawings. Born in Bologna in 1890. After 1918 for a short time he was one of the circle who produced *pittura metafisica*. He found a place of his own as a modern still-life painter. The colours and forms of his pictures suggest the magic harmony of everyday things (*fig. 81*)

Mortensen, Richard. Danish painter.

Born in Copenhagen in 1910. Abstract painter, influenced by Kandinsky. His pictures are the result of a strict disciplining of geometrical form. Works in Paris (*fig. 124*)

Munch, Edvard. Norwegian. Paintings and drawings. Born in Loeiten near Hamar in 1863, died in Ekely near Oslo in 1944. One of the great precursors of Expressionism and also Norway's greatest painter. During the long period when he lived abroad (in Paris, Italy and Germany) he came to know the art of Toulouse Lautrec, van Gogh and Gauguin, who must undoubtedly have influenced him. In his pictures the expression of feeling always dominates and distorts the form and colour (*fig. 28*)

Nay, Ernst Wilhelm. German painter. Born in Berlin in 1902. Abstract painter whose colour rhythm gives him a special place in Abstract painting (*fig. 134*)

Nicholson, Ben. English painter. Born in Denham in 1894. A prominent English Abstract artist whose pictures, puritanical in feeling, reveal a special lyrical attitude towards reality (*fig. 130*)

Nolde, Emil (Emil Hansen). German. Paintings and drawings. Born in Nolde in 1867, died in Seebüll in 1956. A prominent German Expressionist who belonged to the *Brücke* group. He opened up religious horizons to Expressionism. His spontaneous feeling for nature was expressed in strongly coloured, visionary landscape pictures (*fig. 38*)

O'Keeffe, Georgia. American painter. Born in 1887 in Sun Prairie, Wisconsin. Her strictly disciplined pictures are based on reality, which she transforms into almost abstract, hard figures (*fig. 99*)

Orozco, José Clemente. Mexican painter. Born in Zapotlán in 1883, died in Mexico City in 1949. With Rivera and Siqueiros he created present-day Mexican mural painting. His style is strongly mobile and weighted with Expressionistic passion (*fig. 120*)

Permeke, Constant. Belgian painter. Born in Antwerp in 1886, died in Ostend in 1952. He and van den Berghe are the dominant figures in Belgian Expressionism; in his pictures and sculpture his feeling for the earthy power of country life is strongly expressed (*fig. 93*)

Picabia, Francis. French painter of Spanish origin. Born in Paris in 1878, died there in 1953. After a period as a Cubist, which led him to Abstract art, he became the leader of the French Dadaists in 1919 (*fig. 83*)

Picasso, Pablo (Ruiz y Picasso). Spanish. Paintings, drawings, ceramics, etc. Born in Malaga in 1881. At 19 he went to Paris where he at first admired van Gogh and Toulouse Lautrec and soon won for himself a place as the most important, most talked-of painter of the first half of the twentieth century. Associated with Braque and Matisse. After his 'blue' and 'pink' periods his Cubist phase began in 1907. His classical period began in 1917, and in 1925 this alternated with an expressive Surrealistic style. Right up to the present day he has continued all these styles simultaneously, making a rich and vital contribution to the art of today. Lives in the South of France (*figs. 21, 46, 48, 104-5, 169*)

Poliakoff, Serge. French painter. Born in Moscow in 1906. His Abstract pictures are derived from large geometrical figures; nevertheless a clearly perceptible lyrical content vibrates in his handling of shape, colour and material (*fig. 171*)

Pollock, Jackson. American painter. Born in Cody, Wyoming in 1912, died in Southampton, New York in 1956. He was one of the main figures in American Abstract Expressionistic art, and his work had a wide influence. His spontaneous technique, produced by the artist's physical movement spraying and trickling paint – makes him a pioneer of Action Painting (*fig. 143*)

Redon, Odilon. French. Paintings and drawings. Born in Bordeaux in 1840, died in Paris in 1916. He depicted visions and fantasies from a romantic dream-world and was the leading figure in French Symbolism. After the First World War the Surrealists saw him as one of their ancestors (*fig. 16*)

Riopelle, Jean Paul. Canadian painter. Born in Montreal in 1924. Works in

Paris. With his broadly constructed pictures in rich colours he is the leader of Canada's Abstract school (*fig. 161*)

Rivera, Diego. Mexican painter. Born in Guanajuato in 1886, died in Mexico City in 1957. He, Siqueiros and Orozco are the dominant figures in modern Mexican art. The influence of Cubism and Maya and Aztec art led him to a monumental, architectonically constructed style (*fig. 101*)

Rohlfs, Christian. German painter. Born in Niendorf in 1849, died in Hagen in 1938. After many years as a traditional painter he turned to Expressionism in his sixties. His landscapes and townscapes in strong, elementary colours express a lyrical feeling for nature (*fig. 103*)

Rothko, Mark. American painter. Born in Dvinsk, Latvia, in 1903. Has lived in America since 1913. An important Abstract painter with strong colour-expressiveness: large, vibrating patches of colour convey a lyrical feeling for space (*fig. 175*)

Rouault, Georges. French. Paintings and drawings. Born in 1871 in Paris, died there in 1958. One of the greatest painters of the present day. In his pictures the worlds of Goya, Rembrandt and Daumier convey a spiritualized, expressive message. His drawings, etchings, and book illustrations are all of great significance (*fig. 43*)

Rousseau, Henri, called Le Douanier. French painter. Born in Laval in 1844, died in Paris in 1910. This great 'primitive' painter, who began as an amateur, was appreciated by 'real' artists. He was a friend of Gauguin, Redon and Picasso, and his naïve and penetrating painting had an influence on many painters of this century; he is the first 'lay painter' in modern art (*fig. 20*)

Roussel, Ker Xavier. French painter. Born in Lorry-les-Metz in 1867 died in l'Etang-la-Ville in 1944. A friend of Bonnard and Vuillard; like them he belonged to the Nabis group (*fig. 15*)

Schlemmer, Oskar. German painter and sculptor. Born in Stuttgart in 1888, died in Baden-Baden in 1943. Taught at the Bauhaus. The relationships between figures and space are the elements on which Schlemmer's very personal art is built. In their strict discipline his figure compositions approach Abstract art, and his work as a ballet and theatre designer also caused him to turn in this direction (*fig. 70*)

Schmidt-Rottluff, Karl. German. Paintings and drawings. Born at Rottluff near Chemnitz in 1884. One of the leading German Expressionists; founded the *Brücke* group with Kirchner and Heckel. His work is distinguished from that of his friends by its robust construction. (*fig. 37*)

Schumacher, Emil. German painter. Born in Hagen in 1912. An important exponent of Tachism in Germany: the patch-effect, created spontaneously, becomes the subject of the picture (*fig. 147*)

Schwitters, Kurt. German painter. Born in Hanover in 1887, died in Ambleside (England) in 1948. Member of the Dada movement in Germany. He created Abstract collages of the most delicate harmony out of waste material, both as a protest against artistic convention and to create a new order out of the chaos of the different materials (*fig. 77*)

Segall, Lasar. Brazilian painter. Born in Vilna in 1891, died in São Paulo in 1956. Began in Berlin and Dresden as one of the German Expressionists. From 1923 he lived in Brazil where he pioneered modern art. From Expressionist principles he developed a style strongly rooted in simplification, with an almost Abstract vocabulary, but always with markedly social and dramatic themes (*fig. 91*)

Séraphine de Senlis (Séraphine Louis). French painter. Born in Assy in 1864, died in Senlis in 1942. An amateur artist who painted nothing but flowers and fruit (*fig. 108*)

Seurat, Georges. French painter. Born in Paris in 1859, died there in 1891. A Neo-Impressionist who applied the colours to the canvas systematically and scientifically. The way he did this has been called Pointillism, because he built up the colours out of tiny dots of complementary colours. Reacting against Impressionism, his art re-stressed the value of the artistic composition. Hence Seurat is one of the direct ancestors of modern art (*fig. 8*)

Shahn, Ben. American painter. Born in Kovno, Lithuania in 1898. He is one of the most important masters of social criticism in the United States, and notes down his sharp comments clearly and intelligibly in a precise style which, however, only retains what is essential (*fig. 89*)

Sickert, Walter Richard. English painter, son of a Danish painter. Born in Munich in 1860, died in Bath in 1942. Pupil of Whistler's and the most influential English Impressionist; his art approached that of the French Nabis (Bonnard, etc) (*fig. 23*)

Signac, Paul. French painter. Born in 1863 in Paris, died there in 1935. One of the Neo-Impressionists, who began as an Impressionist under the influence of Monet. After Seurat's death he was the leader of the Neo-Impressionist school which continued Seurat's strict discipline with more freedom. A friend of Georges Seurat and Vincent van Gogh. He was also an important theorist whose essays on paintings and painters were a significant contribution to the literature of art (*fig. 10*)

Siqueiros, David Alfaro. Mexican. Paintings and drawings. Born in Chihuahua in 1898. One of the chief masters of Mexican mural painting. His work is distinguished from that of his friends Rivera and Orozco chiefly by its great dynamism (*fig. 121*)

Soulages, Pierre. French painter. Born in Rodez in 1919. Abstract artist, who has created strongly dramatic paintings, full of contrast, out of black marks (*fig. 148*)

Soutine, Chaim. Russian-French painter. Born in Smilovitch in 1894, died in Paris in 1943. For him colour was of the greatest importance and he used it with smouldering passion to produce a deeply tragical expressive effect. In his pictures he derived a new melancholy beauty from decay and confusion (*fig. 42*)

Spala, Vaclav. Czechoslovak painter. Born in Zlutice in 1885, died in Prague in 1946. Spala is the painter who helped the new trends to break through in his country: his art derives both from the construction of Cubism and from the chromatic richness of the Fauves (*fig. 106*)

Spencer, Stanley. English painter. Born in Cookham in 1891, died there in 1959. He is the greatest English *Neue Sachlichkeit* painter and exploited his style to monumental effect in large murals (*fig. 117*)

Staël, Nicolas de. Russian-French painter. Born in Leningrad in 1914, died in Antibes in 1955. One of the most important Abstract painters of the present day; his strongly coloured pictures are built up out of large, architectonically constructed areas. In his late works the lyrical keynote prevails even more strongly, while the colour is almost completely repressed (*fig. 135*)

Sutherland, Graham. English painter and etcher. Born in London in 1903. Starting from natural forms, Sutherland has arrived at a prickly, pointed world of forms whose magical suggestivity is almost on the plane of Surrealism (*fig. 154*)

Tamayo, Rufino. Mexican painter and lithographer. Born in Oaxaca in 1899. Influenced by Cubism and Mexican folk-art, he moved on to a form of mural painting which made its effect with lyrical, subtle nuances, instead of the heaviness and robustness of the earlier Mexican school. (*fig. 155*)

Tanguy, Yves. French painter. Born in Paris in 1900, died in Waterbury, Connecticut, in 1955. A self-taught artist, he began by painting dream-landscapes, then in 1925 he met the Surrealists and became their most original member with his hallucinatory landscapes in which the objects often seem to be undergoing a magic decay (*fig. 84*)

Tapiès, Antonio. Spanish painter. Born in Barcelona in 1923. His art is inspired by the pattern of crumbling walls, etc; he translates the magic life of these forms into an Abstract language almost without colour and with great graphic power (*fig. 174*)

Tobey, Mark. American painter. Born in Centerville, Wisconsin in 1890. Abstract artist of the older generation. Through his contact with the worlds of the Chinese script and Eastern mysticism he arrived at an Abstract rhythm of particularly consistent distinction (fig. 167)

Toorop, Charley. Dutch painter. Born in Katwijk aan Zee in 1891, died in Bergen in 1955. She was an important member of the so-called 'Bergense school', and a very expressive realistic artist (fig. 118)

Utrillo, Maurice. French painter, son of the painter Suzanne Valadon. Born in 1883 in Paris, died at Dax in 1955. Self-taught, with great natural gifts. In his views of Paris streets he extended the intimate charm of the Nabis painting to the sphere of the townscape (fig. 24)

Vallotton, Félix. Swiss. Paintings and drawings. Born in Lausanne in 1865, died in Paris in 1925. He belonged to the Nabis group; he is distinguished from his friends in the Intimist circle by the hardness and dry clarity of his pictures (fig. 19)

Vasarely, Victor. Hungarian painter. Born in Pécs in 1908. Abstract painter who work in Paris. In his pictures, with their strict geometrical construction, manifold visual experience is subordinated to a simple constructive plan (fig. 125)

Velde, Bram van. Dutch painter. Born in Zoeterwoude in 1895. Works in Paris. His large-scale pictures use bright colours to translate a very personal sensibility into a spontaneous language of forms (fig. 170)

Vieira da Silva, Maria Elena. Portuguese-French painter. Born in Lisbon in 1908. The painting of this artist suggests a feeling for space of fantastic dimensions by means of a delicate, subtle network of lines (fig. 166)

Villon, Jacques (Gaston Duchamp). French painter. Born in Damville in 1875. After beginning as an illustrator, in 1911 he joined the Cubists and remained a Cubist consistently. Light and colour have steadily become of greater importance to him (fig. 56)

Vlaminck, Maurice de. French painter. Born in Paris in 1876, died in Paris in 1958. Influenced by van Gogh and later by Cézanne. Painted with unmixed colours. Like André Derain, he was an important Fauvist. His Fauvist painting seems to explode out of his stormy temperament (fig. 34)

Vuillard, Edouard. French. Paintings and drawings. Born in Cuiseaux in 1868, died in La Baule in 1940. Like Bonnard he was a Post-Impressionist and belonged to the Nabis. Vuillard's simple and intimate work with its surprising snatches of reality and its incisive decoration made an important contribution to the development of modern art (figs. 13, 14)

Wagemaker, Jaap. Dutch painter. Born in Haarlem in 1906. Self-taught. In his pictures and montages he uses the material as suggestive means to effect a new feeling for space (fig. 172)

Wiemken, Walter Kurt. Swiss painter. Born in Breggia in 1907, died there in 1941. Early Surrealist (fig. 132)

Winter, Fritz. German painter. Born in 1905 in Altenbögge. Began life as a miner. Studied with Klee and Kandinsky to become one of Germany's important Abstract painters. In his work the melancholy linear structure contrasts with the power of glowing colours (fig. 140)

Wols, Wolfgang (Otto Alfred Schulze-Battman). German painter. Born in Berlin in 1913, died in Paris in 1951. His small, spider's-web-like pictures come from the world of dreams and obsessions. With his spontaneous picture language, rising out of the unconscious, he became a pioneer of Expressive Abstraction (fig. 142)

Wouters, Rik. Belgian painter and sculptor. Born in Malines in 1882, died in Amsterdam in 1916. Influenced by the French Impressionists and Fauves. Even during the severe illness which led to his early death his pictures were a hymn to the joy of life, in glowing colours and very personal, tightly knit structure (fig. 22)

Zaritsky, Joseph. Israeli painter. Born in Borispol in 1891. Works in Israel. Abstract artist who primarily experiments with colour. A pioneer of Abstract art in Israel (fig. 159)

Captions

Captions

1 **Cézanne, Paul,** *In the Forest.* 1895-1900. Oil on canvas, $31\frac{7}{8}$ × $25\frac{5}{8}$ in. Pittsburgh, Pennsylvania: G. David Thompson Collection

2 **Cézanne, Paul,** *Pot and Bottles.* 1900-1906. Water-colour, $8\frac{1}{4}$ × $10\frac{3}{8}$ in. Japan: Matsugata Collection

3 **Gauguin, Paul,** *Annah, the Javanese Girl.* 1893. Oil on canvas, $45\frac{5}{8}$ × $31\frac{7}{8}$ in. Berne: Hahnloser Collection

4 **Gauguin, Paul,** *Les Alyscamps* (*Arles*). 1888. Oil on canvas, 12 × $28\frac{3}{4}$ in. Paris: Louvre (Jeu de Paume)

5 **Gogh, Vincent van,** *The Evening Walk.* 1889, Saint-Rémy period. Oil on canvas, $19\frac{1}{4}$ × $17\frac{3}{4}$ in. São Paulo: Museum

6 **Gogh, Vincent van,** *Thistles.* 1888. Oil on canvas, $23\frac{1}{4}$ × $19\frac{1}{4}$ in. Niarchos Collection

7 **Gogh, Vincent van,** *Young Peasant Girl.* 1890. Auvers period. Oil on canvas, $36\frac{1}{4}$ × $28\frac{3}{4}$ in. Berne: Hahnloser Collection

8 **Seurat, Georges,** *Woman Powdering Herself.* 1889-1890. Oil on canvas, $37\frac{3}{8}$ × $31\frac{1}{8}$ in. London: Courtauld Institute Galleries

9 **Monet, Claude,** *Twilight* (detail). 1908. Oil on canvas, $29\frac{1}{8}$ × $36\frac{5}{8}$ in. Tokyo: Ishibashi Collection

10 **Signac, Paul,** *Woman | Doing Her Hair.* 1893. Encaustic painting on canvas, $23\frac{5}{8}$ × $28\frac{3}{4}$ in. Paris: Mme Cachin-Signac Collection

11 **Bonnard, Pierre,** *Man and Woman.* 1900. Oil on canvas, $44\frac{1}{8}$ × $28\frac{3}{8}$ in. Paris: Musée d'Art Moderne

12 **Bonnard, Pierre,** *Palais de Glace.* 1898. Oil on canvas, $39\frac{3}{8}$ × $29\frac{1}{2}$ in. Berne: Hahnloser Collection

13 **Vuillard, Edouard,** *Sewing.* 1893. Oil on canvas, $15\frac{3}{4}$ × 13 in. Paris: private collection

14 **Vuillard, Edouard,** *Draughts.* 1906. Oil on canvas, $29\frac{7}{8}$ × $42\frac{7}{8}$ in. Berne: Hahnloser Collection

15 **Roussel, Ker Xavier,** *Two Women and Child.* *c* 1891. Oil on canvas, 26 × $21\frac{1}{4}$ in. Paris: Georges Renan Collection

16 **Redon, Odilon,** *The Red Thorns.* *c* 1897-8. Pastel, $20\frac{1}{4}$ × $14\frac{5}{8}$ in. Arles: L. Fayet Collection

17 **Ensor, James,** *Carnival.* 1888. Oil on canvas, $21\frac{1}{4}$ × $28\frac{3}{4}$ in. Amsterdam: Stedelijk Museum

18 **Denis, Maurice,** *Eva in a Green Dress.* 1891. Oil on canvas, $21\frac{7}{8}$ × $13\frac{3}{4}$ in. Private collection

19 **Vallotton, Félix,** *The Maid.* 1902. Oil on canvas, $31\frac{1}{8}$ × $19\frac{1}{4}$ in. Lausanne: Vallotton Collection

20 **Rousseau, Henri, called Le Douanier Rousseau,** *Portrait of Pierre Loti.* 1906. Oil on canvas, $19\frac{5}{8}$ × 24 in. Zurich: Kunsthaus

21 **Picasso, Pablo,** *Seated Saltimbanque with Boy.* 1906. Oil on

canvas, $39\frac{3}{8} \times 27\frac{5}{8}$ in. Zurich: Kunsthaus

22 **Wouters, Rik,** *Snow in March.* 1912. Oil on canvas, $39\frac{3}{8} \times 31\frac{1}{2}$ in. Amsterdam: Stedelijk Museum

23 **Sickert, Walter Richard,** *Nude at the Mirror. c* 1907. Oil on canvas, $25\frac{5}{8} \times 20\frac{1}{2}$ in. London: H. H. Marks Collection

24 **Utrillo, Maurice,** *Eglise de Sainte-Marguerite. c* 1911. Oil on cardboard, $27\frac{1}{4} \times 20\frac{1}{2}$ in. Mannheim: Kunsthalle

25 **Modigliani, Amedeo,** *Portrait of Mme Haydn.* Oil on canvas, $36\frac{1}{4} \times 23\frac{5}{8}$ in. Paris: Musée d'Art Moderne

26 **Modersohn-Becker, Paula,** *Little Girl with Green Necklace.* 1904. Oil on canvas, $21\frac{5}{8} \times 16\frac{1}{2}$ in. Mannheim: Kunsthalle

27 **Corinth, Lovis,** *Landscape of the Walchensee.* 1920. Oil on canvas, $31\frac{1}{8} \times 43\frac{1}{4}$ in. Mannheim: Kunsthalle

28 **Munch, Edvard,** *Summer Night on the Shore of the Oslo Fjord. c* 1900. Oil on canvas, $28\frac{1}{8} \times 39\frac{3}{8}$ in. Mannheim: Kunsthalle

29 **Bonnard, Pierre,** *Nude Washing. c* 1922. Oil on canvas, $46\frac{1}{2} \times 30\frac{3}{4}$ in. Paris: Musée d'Art Moderne

30 **Hodler, Ferdinand,** *The Jungfrau from Mürren.* 1911. Oil on canvas, $34\frac{3}{4} \times 26$ in. Winterthur: Reinhart Foundation

31 **Marquet, Albert,** *The Port of Le Havre. c* 1907. Oil on canvas, $23\frac{5}{8} \times 18\frac{1}{2}$ in. Geneva: private collection

32 **Matisse, Henri,** *Algerian Woman.* 1909. Oil on canvas, $31\frac{1}{2} \times 25\frac{5}{8}$ in. Paris: Musée d'Art Moderne

33 **Matisse, Henri,** *The Bank.* 1907. Oil on canvas, $28\frac{3}{4} \times 23\frac{5}{8}$ in. Basle: Museum

34 **Vlaminck, Maurice de,** *On the Banks of the Seine.* 1906. Oil on canvas, $20\frac{7}{8} \times 25\frac{1}{4}$ in. Zurich: Bührle Collection

35 **Derain, André,** *Seascape, Collioure. c* 1905. Oil on canvas, $17\frac{3}{4} \times 14\frac{5}{8}$ in. Brussels: private collection

36 **Heckel, Erich,** *Nude on a Couch.* 1909. Oil on canvas, $38\frac{5}{8} \times 47\frac{5}{8}$ in. Munich: Bayerische Staatsgemäldesammlungen

37 **Schmidt-Rottluff, Karl,** *Summer Window.* 1912. Oil on canvas, $44\frac{1}{4} \times 34\frac{5}{8}$ in. Mannheim: Kunsthalle

38 **Nolde, Emil (Hansen),** *Flame Lilies and Dark Delphiniums. c* 1915. Oil on canvas, $28\frac{3}{4} \times 34\frac{5}{8}$ in. Mannheim: Kunsthalle

39 **Kirchner, Ernst Ludwig,** *Nude Girl Behind a Curtain.* 1909. Oil on canvas, $47\frac{1}{4} \times 35\frac{5}{8}$ in. Amsterdam: Stedelijk Museum

40 **Dufy, Raoul,** *In the Garden.* 1905. Oil on canvas, $35\frac{3}{4} \times 33\frac{7}{8}$ in. New York: Rosensaft Collection

41 **Jawlensky, Alexej von,** *Hard Winter.* 1916. Oil on canvas, $14\frac{1}{8} \times 10\frac{5}{8}$ in. Basle: Museum

42 **Soutine, Chaim,** *Flayed Ox. c* 1925. Oil on canvas, $28\frac{1}{2} \times 19\frac{5}{8}$ in. Switzerland: private collection

43 **Rouault, Georges,** *Female Nude.* 1906. Water-colour, $11 \times 8\frac{5}{8}$ in. Niarchos Collection

44 **Kokoschka, Oskar,** *Portrait of a Little Girl.* 1913. Oil on canvas, $36\frac{3}{4} \times 27\frac{3}{4}$ in. Mannheim: Kunsthalle

45 **Dongen, Kees van,** *Moroccan Women at Cap Spartel.* 1910. Oil on canvas, $21\frac{5}{8} \times 15$ in. Artist's Collection

46 **Picasso, Pablo,** *Loaves and Fruit-Dish on a Table.* 1908. Oil on canvas, $64\frac{5}{8} \times 52\frac{1}{8}$ in. Basle: Museum

47 **Braque, Georges,** *The Sacré Coeur Seen from the Artist's Studio.* 1910. Oil on canvas, $21\frac{1}{4} \times 15\frac{7}{8}$ in. Roubaix: private collection

48 **Picasso, Pablo,** *Bottle, Flute, Violin, Newspaper, Glass.* 1914. Oil on canvas, $21\frac{5}{8} \times 18\frac{1}{8}$ in. Switzerland, private collection

49 **Braque, Georges,** *Still-Life, 'Melody'.* 1914. Oil on canvas, $21\frac{5}{8} \times 15$ in. Paris: private collection

50 **La Fresnaye, Roger de,** *14 July.*

1914. Oil on canvas, 44⅞ × 57⅛ in. Paris: Musée d'Art Moderne

51 **Gris, Juan,** *Fruit-Dish and Carafe.* 1914. Sized paper, charcoal and oil on canvas, 36¼ × 25⅝ in. Otterlo: Kröller-Müller Museum

52 **Duchamp, Marcel,** *The Chess-Players.* 1911. Oil on canvas, 19⅝ × 24 in. Paris: Musée d'Art Moderne

53 **Boccioni, Umberto,** *Dynamism of a Cyclist.* 1913. Oil on canvas, 27⅜ × 37⅜ in. Milan: Mattioli Collection

54 **Carrà, Carlo,** *Portrait of F. T. Marinetti.* Oil on canvas, 35⅜ × 31½ in. Rome: Marinetti Collection

55 **Ballà, Giacomo,** *Racing Car, Abstract Speed.* 1913. Water-colour and Indian ink, paper, canvas, 27⅝ × 39⅜ in. Amsterdam: Stedelijk Museum

56 **Villon, Jacques,** *The Wrestlers.* 1937. Oil on canvas, 36⅝ × 29⅛ in. Paris: Musée d'Art Moderne

57 **Larionov, Michail,** *Portrait.* c 1911. Oil on canvas, 40⅛ × 33⅛ in. Paris: Musée d'Art Moderne

58 **Léger, Fernand,** *The Wedding.* 1911-12. Oil on canvas 101⅛ × 81⅛ in. Paris: Musée d'Art Moderne

59 **Delaunay, Robert,** *The Eiffel Tower.* 1910. Oil on canvas, 76⅞ × 50¾ in. Basle: Museum

60 **Macke, August,** *Landscape.* 1914. Water-colour, 8⅜ × 9½ in. Lausanne: Breguet Collection

61 **Campendonk, Heinrich,** *Man with Flower.* 1918. Oil on canvas, 23⅝ × 23 in. Amsterdam: Stedelijk Museum

62 **Marc, Franz,** *Two Cats.* 1912. Oil on canvas, 29¼ × 38⅝ in. Basle: Museum

63 **Chagall, Marc,** *Double Portrait with Glass of Wine.* 1917. Oil on canvas, 91¾ × 53½ in. Paris: Musée d'Art Moderne

64 **Chagall, Marc,** *The Grey House.* 1917. Oil on canvas, 26¾ × 29⅛ in. Brussels: private collection

65 **Klee, Paul,** *Puppet Theatre.* 1923. Water-colour on gesso ground, 21½ × 14¾ in. Berne: Klee Foundation

66 **Klee, Paul,** *The Oracle.* 1922-3. Oil on cardboard on wood, 19¾ × 20¼ in. Basle: Galerie Beyeler

67 **Kandinsky, Wassilij,** *Large Nude.* 1911. Oil on canvas, 58 × 39 in. Basle: Galerie Beyeler

68 **Kandinsky, Wassilij,** *Black Patch.* 1921. Oil on canvas, 53⅞ × 47¼ in. Zurich: Kunsthaus

69 **Kupka, Frank,** *Vertical Planes.* 1912-13. Oil on canvas, 39 × 26¾ in. Paris: Musée d'Art Moderne

70 **Schlemmer, Oskar,** *Scene at Table.* 1923. Oil on paper, 24⅞ × 19¾ in. Mannheim: Kunsthalle

71 **Feininger, Lyonel,** *Church in the Market-Place.* 1929. Oil on canvas, 39⅜ × 31½ in. Mannheim: Kunsthalle

72 **Malewitsch, Kasimir,** *The Woodcutter.* 1911. Oil on canvas, 37 × 28⅛ in. Amsterdam: Stedelijk Museum

73 **Malewitsch, Kasimir,** *Eight Red Rectangles.* After 1914. Oil on canvas, 22⅝ × 19 in. Amsterdam: Stedelijk Museum

74 **Doesburg, Theo van.** *The Card-Players.* 1916-17. Oil on canvas, 45⅝ × 41¾ in. The Hague: Municipal Museum

75 **Leck, Bart van der,** *The Rider.* 1918. Oil on canvas, 37 × 15¾ in. Otterlo: Kröller-Müller Museum

76 **Mondriaan, Piet,** *Composition.* 1921. Oil on canvas, 19⅜ × 16¼ in. Basle: Museum

77 **Schwitters, Kurt,** *Dislocated Forces.* 1920. Collage, montage and oil on canvas, 41⅞ × 34 in. Berne: Huggler Collection

78 **Lissitzky, El,** *Proun.* Oil on canvas, 24⅜ × 19⅝ in. Steinhude am Meer: Dr Hermann Bode Collection

79 **Léger, Fernand,** *Women in an Interior.* 1922. Oil on canvas, 24¾ × 21¼ in. Paris: Musée d'Art Moderne

80 **Chirico, Giorgio de**, *Still-Life in a Landscape*. 1915. Oil on canvas, $31\frac{7}{8} \times 25\frac{5}{8}$ in. Brussels: Mabille Collection

81 **Morandi, Giorgio**, *Still-Life*. 1916. Oil on canvas, $21\frac{1}{4} \times 23\frac{5}{8}$ in. Milan: Mattioli Collection

82 **Campigli, Massimo**, *The Guardian*. 1929. Oil on canvas, $36\frac{1}{4} \times 23\frac{5}{8}$ in. Milan: Mattioli Collection

83 **Picabia, Francis**, *Udnie (American Girl, or the Dance)*. 1913. Oil on canvas, $118\frac{1}{8} \times 118\frac{1}{8}$ in. Paris: Musée d'Art Moderne

84 **Tanguy, Yves**, *Le Palais aux Rochers de Fenêtres*. 1942. Oil on canvas, 64×52 in. Paris: Musée d'Art Moderne

85 **Dali, Salvador**, *The Giraffe on Fire*. 1935 (?). Oil on panel, $13\frac{3}{4} \times 10\frac{5}{8}$ in. Basle: Museum

86 **Delvaux, Paul**, *Jeux de Mains*. 1941. Oil on canvas, $29\frac{1}{2} \times 43\frac{1}{4}$ in. Beersel: Madame la Baronne de Hauteville Collection

87 **Magritte, René**, *On the Threshold of Liberty*. 1929. Oil on canvas, $44\frac{7}{8} \times 57\frac{1}{2}$ in. Brussels: Urvater Collection

88 **Ernst, Max**, *Après Moi le Sommeil (After Me - Sleep)*. 1958. Oil on canvas, $51\frac{1}{8} \times 34\frac{5}{8}$ in. Paris: Musée d'Art Moderne

89 **Shahn, Ben**, *The Physicist*. 1961. Tempera on canvas, $31\frac{1}{2} \times 52$ in. New York: Jack Lawrence Collection/Lawrence-Myden Foundation

90 **Lurçat, Jean**, *Masts and Sails*. 1930. Oil on canvas, $47\frac{7}{8} \times 56\frac{5}{8}$ in. Amsterdam: Stedelijk Museum

91 **Segall, Lasar**, *Self-Portrait*. 1919. Oil on canvas. Munich: Helene Spitzer Collection

92 **Berghe, Frits van den**, *Genealogy*. 1929. Oil on canvas, $57\frac{1}{2} \times 44\frac{1}{2}$ in. Basle: Museum

93 **Permeke, Constant**, *View over Aertrijke*. Oil on canvas, $39\frac{5}{8} \times 47\frac{1}{4}$. Amsterdam: Stedelijk Museum

94 **Dunoyer de Segonzac, André**, *Grimaud*. Water-colour, $29\frac{1}{2} \times 21\frac{5}{8}$ in. Geneva: Robert Rey Collection

95 **Legueult, Raymond-Jean**, *Young Woman in the Garden*. 1951. Oil on canvas, $36\frac{1}{4} \times 25\frac{5}{8}$ in. Paris: Dr Fossez Collection

96 **Auberjonois, René**, *Still-Life with Guitar*. 1940. Oil on canvas, $18\frac{7}{8} \times 15\frac{3}{8}$ in. Lausanne: private collection

97 **Gromaire, Marcel**, *Reading Her Palm*. 1935. Oil on canvas, $39\frac{3}{8} \times 31\frac{7}{8}$ in. Paris: Musée d'Art Moderne

98 **Marin, John**, *Lower Manhattan*. 1920. Water-colour. $21\frac{1}{4} \times 28$ in. New York: Museum of Modern Art, Philip L. Goodwin Collection

99 **O'Keeffe, Georgia**, *From the Plain*. 1954. Oil on canvas, 72×48 in. New York: David Workman Collection

100 **Beckmann, Max**, *Pierrette and a Clown*. 1925. Oil on canvas, $63 \times 39\frac{3}{8}$ in. Mannheim: Kunsthalle

101 **Rivera, Diego**, *The Flower-Sellers*. 1943. Oil on canvas. Mexico: Valdès Collection

102 **Gaillard, Christian**, *Arab Girl in White*. 1955. Oil on canvas, $36\frac{1}{4} \times 28\frac{3}{4}$ in. Paris: private collection

103 **Rohlfs, Christian**, *Church at Soest*. 1918. Tempera on canvas, $39\frac{3}{8} \times 24$ in. Mannheim: Kunsthalle

104-5 **Picasso, Pablo**, *The Charnel-House*. 1944-5. Oil on canvas, $78\frac{3}{4} \times 98\frac{3}{8}$ in. New York: Walter P. Chrysler Jr Collection

106 **Spala, Vaclav**, *Two Women Washing*. 1937. Oil on canvas, $33\frac{1}{4} \times 28\frac{3}{4}$ in. Private collection

107 **Makovski, Tadeusz**, *The Painter – Portrait of the Artist*. 1929. Oil on canvas, $36\frac{1}{4} \times 28\frac{3}{4}$ in. Paris: Musée d'Art Moderne

108 **Séraphine**, *The Tree of Paradise*. 1929. Oil on canvas, $76\frac{1}{4} \times 50\frac{3}{4}$ in. Paris: Musée d'Art Moderne

109 **Bombois, Camille,** *Chartres.* c 1925. Oil on canvas, $28\frac{3}{4} \times 23\frac{5}{8}$ in Paris: private collection
110 **Kruyder, Herman,** *The Cock.* 1933–4. Oil on canvas, $42\frac{1}{2} \times 48\frac{3}{8}$ in. Amsterdam: Stedelijk Museum
111 **Brusselmans, Jean,** *Apple-Trees in Blossom.* 1931. Oil on canvas, $43\frac{1}{4} \times 51\frac{1}{8}$ in. Courtrai: Herbert Collection
112 **Mirò, Joan,** *Figures and Dog in Front of the Sun.* 1949. Tempera on canvas, $31\frac{7}{8} \times 21\frac{1}{4}$ in. Basle: Museum
113 **Marchand, André,** *Morning in the Port.* 1960. Oil on canvas, $25\frac{5}{8} \times 31\frac{7}{8}$ in. Geneva: private collection
114 **Generalič, Ivan,** *Funeral of Stef Halacek.* 1934. Oil on canvas, $19\frac{5}{8} \times 18\frac{1}{2}$ in. Zagreb: Galerie Galenje
115 **Bauchant, André,** *Louis XI Having Mulberry-Trees Planted outside Tours.* 1943. Oil on canvas on panel, $74\frac{3}{4} \times 40\frac{1}{8}$ in. Paris: Musée d'Art Moderne
116 **Dix, Otto,** *Portrait of His Parents.* 1924. Oil on canvas, $47\frac{1}{8} \times 52$ in. Hanover: Städtische Galerie im Landesmuseum
117 **Spencer, Stanley,** *Self-Portrait.* 1936. Oil on canvas, $24\frac{1}{8} \times 18\frac{1}{8}$ in. Amsterdam: Stedelijk Museum
118 **Toorop, Charley,** *Cheese Market, Alkmaar.* 1932–3. Oil on canvas, $59 \times 70\frac{7}{8}$ in. Amsterdam: Stedelijk Museum
119 **Guttuso, Renato,** *Nude on the Line.* 1959. Oil on canvas, $47\frac{1}{4} \times 23\frac{5}{8}$ in. Private collection
120 **Orozco, José Clemente,** *Zapatisias.* 1931. Oil on canvas, $44\frac{7}{8} \times 55\frac{1}{8}$ in. New York: Museum of Modern Art
121 **Siqueiros, David Alfaro,** *Echo of a Cry.* 1937. Duco on panel, $48 \times 35\frac{7}{8}$ in. New York: Museum of Modern Art
122 **Mondriaan, Piet,** *Composition in Red, Yellow and Blue.* 1939–42. Oil on canvas, $28\frac{3}{8} \times 27\frac{1}{8}$ in. New York: Mrs Donald Ogden Stewart Collection
123 **Domela, César,** *Composition with Transparent Planes.* 1930. Brass, plexiglas, oil, $33\frac{1}{2} \times 33\frac{1}{2}$ in. The Hague: Municipal Museum
124 **Mortensen, Richard,** *Evisa.* 1960. Oil on canvas, $76\frac{3}{4} \times 51\frac{1}{8}$ in. Paris: Galerie Denise Renée
125 **Vasarely, Victor,** *Siris II.* 1954. Oil on canvas, $7\frac{1}{8} \times 11$ in. Paris: Galerie Denise Renée
126 **Kandinsky, Wassilij,** *Seven.* 1943. Oil on cardboard, $22\frac{7}{8} \times 16\frac{7}{8}$ in. Zurich: Max Bill Collection
127 **Magnelli, Alberto,** *Oceanic Round.* 1933. Oil on canvas, $68\frac{1}{2} \times 57\frac{1}{2}$ in. Paris: Musée d'Art Moderne
128 **Braque, Georges,** *The Bike.* 1952. Oil on canvas, $52\frac{3}{8} \times 30\frac{3}{4}$ in. New York: Rosensaft Collection
129 **Lubarda, Petar,** *Rhapsody in Blue.* 1955. Oil on canvas, $31\frac{1}{2} \times 39\frac{3}{8}$ in. Private collection
130 **Nicholson, Ben,** *Stone, Yellow and White.* 1958. Oil on canvas, $30 \times 29\frac{7}{8}$ in. Mannheim: Kunsthalle
131 **Baumeister, Willi,** *Montaru III.* 1953. Oil on pevatex, $39\frac{3}{8} \times 51\frac{1}{8}$ in. Mannheim: Kunsthalle
132 **Wiemken, Walter Kurt,** *All in All.* 1934. Oil on canvas, $63 \times 39\frac{1}{2}$ in. Basle: Museum
133 **Benner, Gerrit,** *The Village.* 1954. Oil on canvas, $23\frac{5}{8} \times 31\frac{1}{2}$ in. Amsterdam: Stedelijk Museum
134 **Nay, Ernst Wilhelm,** *Oasis.* 1952. Oil on canvas, $39\frac{3}{8} \times 47\frac{1}{4}$ in. Mannheim: Kunsthalle
135 **Staël, Nicolas de,** *Abstract Composition.* 1949. Oil on canvas, $63\frac{3}{4} \times 44\frac{7}{8}$ in. Paris: Musée d'Art Moderne
136 **Afro,** *Silver Dollar Club.* 1912. Oil on canvas, $43 \times 79\frac{5}{8}$ in. Milan: Dr E. Jesi Collection
137 **Manessier, Alfred,** *The Crown*

of Thorns. 1950. Oil on canvas, 64⅛ × 38⅝ in. Paris: Musée d'Art Moderne

138 **Bazaine, Jean,** *Landscape*. 1951. Oil on canvas, 36¼ × 28¾ in. Lausanne: private collection

139 **Bissière, Roger,** *Still-Life with Bottles*. 1948. Oil on canvas, 25⅝ × 17¾ in. Paris: Musée d'Art Moderne

140 **Winter, Fritz,** *Nuptial Rain*. 1952. Oil on canvas, 37⅜ × 51⅝ in. Cologne: Wallraf-Richartz Museum

141 **Hartung, Hans,** *Composition*. 1950. Oil on canvas, 15 × 39⅜ in. Geneva: Galerie Benador

142 **Wols, Wolfgang,** *TangledMasts*. 1947. Water-colour on paper, 7¼ × 5⅜ in. Paris: Galerie Europa

143 **Pollock, Jackson,** *Full Fathom Five*. 1947. Oil on canvas, 50¾ × 30 in. New York: Museum of Modern Art (gift of Peggy Guggenheim)

144 **Klee, Paul,** *Saint at a Window*. 1940. Water-colour, 13¾ × 8⅛ in. Berne: Klee Foundation

145 **Corneille,** *Away from the Paths*. 1960. Oil on canvas, 76¾ × 51⅛ in. The Hague: Municipal Museum

146 **Fautrier, Jean,** *The Olive-Trees*. 1957. Oil on canvas, 39⅜ × 51⅛ in. Geneva: Chauvet Collection

147 **Schumacher, Emil,** *Barabbas*. 1958. Oil on canvas, 55⅛ × 37¾ in. Bochum: Städtische Kunstsammlungen

148 **Soulages, Pierre,** *Painting*. 1954. Oil on canvas, 39¾ × 28½ in. Mannheim: Kunsthalle

149 **Kline, Franz,** *Siegfried*. 1958. Oil on canvas, 103⅛ × 81⅛ in. Pittsburgh: Carnegie Institute

150 **Kooning, Willem de,** *Woman IV*. 1953. Oil on canvas, 68⅞ × 79⅛ in. Kansas City: Nelson Gallery, Atkins Museum (gift of William Inge)

151 **Dubuffet, Jean,** *Jardin de Fouille Roucoule*. 1955. Bits of canvas stuck on canvas, 45⅝ × 34⅝ in. Paris: Baron Elie de Rothschild Collection

152 **Buffet, Bernard,** *Bible, Candlestick and Vase of Flowers*. 1956. Oil on canvas, 28¾ × 19⅝ in. Basle: Galerie Beyeler

153 **Bacon, Francis,** *Self-Portrait*. 1956. Oil on canvas, 78 × 53⅞ in. London: Marlborough Fine Art Ltd

154 **Sutherland, Graham,** *Thorn-Tree*. 1945. Oil on canvas, 25⅝ × 20⅛ in. Sir Kenneth Clark Collection

155 **Tamayo, Rufino,** *Women*. 1960. Oil on canvas, 47⅝ × 77⅛ in. Paris: Galerie de France

156 **Lam, Wifredo,** *The Jungle*. 1943. Gouache, paper, canvas, 94½ × 91 in. New York: Museum of Modern Art (Inter-American Fund)

157 **Matta, Roberto Echaurren,** *Listen to Living* (*Ecoutez Vivre*). 1941. Oil on canvas, 29½ × 37⅜ in. New York: Museum of Modern Art (Inter-American Fund)

158 **Gorky, Arshile,** *Study for Agony*. *c* 1947. Oil on canvas, 28 × 38⅛ in. New York: private collection (by courtesy of the Sidney Janis Gallery)

159 **Zaritsky, Joseph.** *Long Live the People, No 2*. 19[illegible]2. Oil on canvas, 78⅜ × 11[illegible]⅞ in. Artist's Collection

160 **Borduas, Paul-Emil,** *Red-Black Composition*. 1959. Oil on canvas, 30⅞ × 38¾ in. Amsterdam: Stedelijk Museum (Sandbergh Collection)

161 **Riopelle, Jean-Paul,** *Chevreuse*. 1960. Oil on canvas, 117⅜ × 149¾ in. Paris: Musée d'Art Moderne

162 **Jorn, Asger,** *The Bridge*. 1957. Oil on canvas, 51⅛ × 38⅛ in. Hengelo, Holland: Mr and Mrs de Jong Collection

163 **Appel, Karel,** *Tragic Nude*. 1956. Oil on canvas, 57½ × 44⅞ in. Eindhoven: Stedelijk van Abbe Museum

164 **Léger, Fernand,** *The Builders*.

1950. Oil on canvas, 118$\frac{1}{8}$ × 78$\frac{3}{4}$ in. Paris: Madame F. Léger Collection

165 **Matisse, Henri,** *The Green Stockings*. 1952. Gouache, 102$\frac{3}{8}$ × 66$\frac{1}{8}$ in. Paris: Mme Duthuit-Matisse Collection

166 **Vieira da Silva, Maria Elena,** *Composition*. 1956. Oil on canvas, 13$\frac{3}{4}$ × 10$\frac{5}{8}$ in. Geneva: Galerie Motte

167 **Tobey, Mark,** *Autumn*. 1960. Tempera on paper, 6$\frac{3}{4}$ × 4$\frac{7}{8}$ in. Paris: Galerie Jeanne Bûcher

168 **Beckmann, Max,** *Removal of the Sphinxes*. 1945. Oil on canvas, 51$\frac{1}{8}$ × 54$\frac{7}{8}$ in. Amsterdam: private collection

169 **Picasso, Pablo,** *Portrait of a Painter, after El Greco*. 1950. Oil on canvas, 39$\frac{1}{2}$ × 31$\frac{7}{8}$ in. Lucerne: Rosengart Collection

170 **Velde, Bram van,** *Composition*.

1946. Gouache on paper, 47$\frac{1}{4}$ × 49$\frac{5}{8}$ in. Paris: Galerie Knoedler

171 **Poliakoff, Serge,** *Composition*. *c* 1960. Oil on canvas, 39$\frac{3}{8}$ × 31$\frac{7}{8}$ in. Lausanne: Galerie Bonnier

172 **Wagemaker, Jaap,** *Tribute to Brassaï*. 1961. Oil, iron, wood, 56$\frac{3}{4}$ × 48 in. Brussels: Philippe Dotremont Collection

173 **Burri, Alberto,** *Grande Ferro*. 1959. Iron, 78$\frac{3}{4}$ × 75$\frac{1}{4}$ in. Milan: Galleria Blu

174 **Tapies, Antonio,** *Grey-Black with Red Cuts*. 1962. Oil on canvas. Paris: Galerie Stadler

175 **Rothko, Mark,** *Red, White and Brown*. 1957. Oil on canvas, 99$\frac{3}{8}$ × 81$\frac{5}{8}$ in. Basle: Musée des Beaux-Arts

176 **Ardon, Mordechai,** *Landscape with Black Sun*. 1961. Oil on canvas, 41$\frac{3}{4}$ × 57$\frac{1}{2}$ in. London: Marlborough Fine Art Ltd